the bridesmaid handbook

sharon naylor

SOURCEBOOKS, INC.
NAPERVILLE, ILLINOIS

Published by Sourcebooks, Inc.
P.O. Box 4410, Naperville, Illinois 60567-4410
(630) 961-3900
FAX: (630) 961-2168
www.sourcebooks.com

Naylor, Sharon.
  The bridesmaid handbook / Sharon Naylor.
      p. cm.
  Includes index.
  ISBN 1-4022-0356-X (alk. paper)
  1. Bridesmaids. 2. Weddings—Planning. 3. Wedding etiquette.
I. Title.

BJ2065.W43N39 2005
395.2'2--dc22

2004026862
ISBN 1-4022-0356-X

Printed and bound in the United States of America
        PX 10 9 8 7 6 5 4 3 2 1

For Jill, Jennifer, Pam, and Loretta

Contents

Acknowledgments

With many thanks to Deb Werksman, Morgan Hrejsa and Kelly Barrales-Saylor for their editing expertise; Tom Todd and the entire Sourcebooks, Inc. team for their tireless dedication to getting the word out on my books; my very dedicated (and very patient) agent Meredith Bernstein for being "The Seer"; and to my publicist Scott Buhrmaster who renews my faith in humanity every day (Scott, I *so* owe you a martini!).

Also, cheers to my friends and bridesmaids Jennifer, Jill, Loretta, Patty, Kathy, Denise, and all of my friends who have lifted up appletinis to toast our collective great fortune of knowing one another.

Introduction

Congratulations on being named a bridesmaid! This means the bride holds you dear to her heart, you're one of her favorite people, and she's chosen you as a very important part of her wedding day. Isn't it great to be so loved?

Now, before your smile fades and your shoulders tense up when the thought hits—*Hey, this is going to be a lot of work, it's going to be expensive, and I might have to wear a peach dress*—just stick with the positives for right now:

- You will become a part of her wedding day memories forever and a permanent part of her life history.
- You were chosen because she trusts you; you're one of the most dependable people she knows. You'll keep her confidences, you'll be there when she needs you, and you'll save the day for her over and over again.
- She knows you have a great perspective on life. You'll have a lighthearted approach even when things go wrong, and you'll get her to not take herself so seriously.

- She knows you're going to make this whole thing fun. If anyone can make her laugh when she most needs it, it's you. If anyone can make the party fabulous, it's you. If anyone can get the dance floor filled, it's you.
- Her kids are going to look at her wedding day pictures someday, point to you, and hear all about how you've been so special to her all of her life.
- You have a long and laugh-filled history with the bride. You're a part of who she is, and you've been there every step of the way with her. Your being a bridesmaid is a thank-you for your important presence in her life so far and also a welcome into her future. You'll be there every step of the way too.
- And if you're single, you get first pick of the handsome, single *groomsmen* at the wedding.

Isn't it great to be a Chosen One? Well, hang on to this happy feeling and be ready to call it up many times in the future when things get stressful. The coming months may turn into a whirlwind of ever-growing expenses, diva co-bridesmaids (who suck the life out of everyone around them), endless shopping excursions, micromanaging mothers, and a bride who gets so overwhelmed she's snapping at you. Oh, and yes, the threat of having to wear a puffy peach dress.

"Wait, Why Did I Say Yes?"

It's amazing how something as happy as planning a wedding can turn into a drama-fest. People sometimes completely lose their minds over the colors of napkins and the icing on the cake. Emotions rise, everyone is bickering, and the bride is in tears. It's enough to make a bridesmaid wonder why she said "Yes" to the invitation—if not how she can now say "No, thanks."

While it's true that some wedding parties get truly out of control, those are in the minority. They're just the ones you hear about more often.

Your situation is going to be different.

I know that's quite a claim to make, since you can't control other people's behavior and stress levels, but let me tell you why you have a better chance of enjoying the entire process: With the help of this book, you're going to be a big reason why everything goes smoothly and everyone enjoys the wedding more. You'll be the one reminding everyone to keep the bigger picture in mind—that it's all about the bride and groom's happiness.

You'll learn how to smoothly and gracefully sweep away any (potential) problems, how to make everything more special, meaningful, and sentimental for the bride and groom. You'll be organized and in the know with the help of this book, taking a lot of pressure off the bride. And you'll be there to give the bride the best gift of all—a reminder of who she is outside of being the bride-to-be so that she doesn't

get lost in the whirlwind. That makes you priceless—
that makes you the dream bridesmaid.

Ready to step into the world of engagement parties, showers, dress shopping, shoe shopping, gift
shopping, bachelorette parties, and all the *excitement*
that comes from being a bridesmaid? Ready to look
fabulous at the wedding? Let's get started…

Part One

The First Steps

What's On Your "To Do" List: The Roles and Responsibilities of Bridesmaids

While the promise of dresses and shoes and fabulous parties and hot groomsmen are the perks of being a bridesmaid, there's a job description underneath it all. You have roles and responsibilities to handle as well. But don't worry—the list is nowhere near as long as the bride and groom's list of "Things To Do." At the end of this chapter, you'll find the *new* responsibilities of today's bridesmaid. Your list is a snap.

THE "TO DO" LIST FOR BRIDESMAIDS

In the past, when weddings were pretty much cookie-cutter and all wedding parties did the same things (just in different color dresses and different degrees of poufiness), bridesmaids did little more than show up to parties and dress-shopping trips, plan a shower, get a gift, and show up for the wedding.

And perhaps lead a conga line at the reception. Sure, they lent moral support to the bride, helped make wedding favors, had their nails and hair done before the wedding, and posed for pictures. They handled those roles well, but today's wedding has changed.

Brides and grooms are no longer having the cookie-cutter wedding. They're all about personalizing, bringing in their shared interests and cultures with theme weddings. They may plan a destination wedding where you'll all fly to St. Lucia for the week. Every one of you may live in a different state or country, since we live in a global society and people move away for work or love. And everyone is *busy*, time-crunched, stressed, with already full schedules, and lots of responsibilities. With these new conditions and with everything in the wedding plans being so unique, it only stands to follow that your Bridesmaid "to do" list can be a bit unique as well.

One bridesmaid from Orlando wrote in to say that part of her "assignment list" was tracking down a place to rent a chocolate fountain. Another bridesmaid from Los Angeles set out to find a stretch Humvee to transport the bridal party on the wedding day as a favor to the bride.

Clearly, the bride and groom are likely to delegate out some of their own tasks, giving you a challenge and a big victory when you find that chocolate fountain or that stretch Humvee. For now, let's look at the traditional, perennial roles that haven't changed very much in the past few decades.

- Attend the engagement party, if one is held, and bring a gift.
- Make time to attend an initial planning meeting (and cocktails!) with the bride and the other bridesmaids. This first meeting sets the stage for the entire planning process to come. This is where you'll find out what the bride has in mind for the wedding, the date and season, the location, the style and formality, the theme, the size, all the basics. (Distance Alert! When everyone lives far apart, this info may come in a detailed email from the bride.)
- Offer to help the bride with any pre-planning or specialty tasks to which you can contribute. (For example, now's the time to tell her your cousin is the head of catering at a great ballroom and can give her a 50 percent discount.)
- Make your travel plans if you need to fly or drive in for the wedding activities.
- Join in the shopping trip for bridesmaids' dresses, shoes, and accessories. Be ready to pay for your own wardrobe and to leave a deposit right now.
- Assist the bride on her own shopping and scouting trips, if asked.
- Help plan and pay for the bridal shower with the Maid of Honor and other bridesmaids.

- Help choose and pay for a bridal shower gift, either as a group gift with the others or just from you.
- Share hostessing duties at the bridal shower, including running games, serving, assisting the bride with her gifts, keeping record of gifts, making the "bow bouquet," and of course, cleanup.
- Attend additional showers given by others if distance allows.
- Attend dress fittings and pay the balance for your dress.
- Attend bridesmaid brunches and other planning meetings.
- Plan, pay for, and co-host the bachelorette party.
- Select and pay for a wedding gift for the couple, wrap it, and fill out a terrific card for them.
- Attend the rehearsal and rehearsal dinner; show up on time and be ready to learn! There's plenty of time to socialize at the reception.
- Show up on time the morning of the wedding, ready for the hair and makeup trip to the salon, and dressed in time for prewedding photos.
- If necessary, show up even earlier to help set up and decorate the wedding site, or help set up breakfast or snacks at the bride's house before you get ready.
- Help the bride get ready.
- Volunteer for last-minute errands, such as picking up a bridesmaid whose car battery is dead, running out to buy extra stockings, or bringing a card to the groom from the bride.

- Complete all duties during the ceremony, following directions, perhaps doing readings or musical performances if asked.
- Stand in the receiving line and make introductions.
- Pose for postwedding pictures.
- Attend the cocktail party and reception, jump-starting the dancing and getting others onto the dance floor. Dance with your appointed groomsman for the first dance, and then choose your date or other partners for other dances.
- Participate in special reception moments, like the throwing of the bouquet or special ethnic dances and rituals.
- Help with end-of-party responsibilities like getting drunk guests safe rides home, transporting all those wedding gifts back to the bride and groom's house, and making sure nothing has been left behind.
- All the way through, be there for whatever the bride needs and whenever she wants to talk.

When You're the Maid (or Matron) of Honor

The list of responsibilities you just read are yours as well, only you'll most likely be taking a leading role in steps like planning the shower and selecting dresses. The Maid of Honor (or Matron of Honor, if you're married) is the bride's Right-Hand

Woman, not necessarily the "boss" of the bridal party but definitely the team leader. Here's a list of what you most likely will do for the wedding:

- Attend the bride's gown shopping excursions as her trusted advisor because she knows you will let her know if a gown isn't flattering on her. Many times, the bride just brings her Maid of Honor for initial gown hunt trips, not wanting too many opinions until she has narrowed down her choices.
- Help the bride keep track of which gowns she tried on where.
- Organize the bridesmaids' own gown orders and payment, including getting size cards from out-of-town bridesmaids.
- Keep all bridesmaids informed about meetings, fittings, gown payment deadlines, shoe orders, and so on.
- Field bridesmaids' questions.
- Take the leading role in planning the bridal shower, but wisely share the decision-making process and the legwork with the other maids.
- Host the bridal shower and make sure all goes smoothly.
- Help the bride record which gifts came from which guests at the bridal shower.
- Help the bride get ready on the morning of the wedding.
- Propose a toast at the rehearsal dinner and at the reception, if you wish.
- Be there for anything the bride needs on the wedding day.

Your Additional Titles

Here's where your job as a bridesmaid gets a bit deeper. It's not just "plan a party, show up." This is where being a friend or a sister comes into play, where you contribute your comfort, loyalty, sense of humor, perspective, and life's wisdom to help the bride in the most important ways possible: by being *you*. Check out the following "job descriptions."

Confidence Keeper. The bride is going to have a lot going on in her mind during this entire process. She's going to be excited, but she's also going to be overwhelmed and pushed to the edge sometimes. She may want to cry, complain, or vent—and that's the best thing she can do so that she doesn't bottle up and fall apart. She needs someone trustworthy to whom she can talk about her fears, and she needs someone she knows would never gossip about her momentary doubts about marriage in general. She needs a safe place to blow off steam or a good listener to help her sort out her feelings...and that would be you.

Martini Maker. Sometimes being a good friend means knowing when it's time to pull out those martini glasses. Whether it's to celebrate the bride's finally finding that perfect gown after fifteen scouting trips, or to blow off steam when the groom's mother says just the wrong thing at the wrong time— drinks are served! Or maybe you'll be the one to plan regular girls' nights out for laughter, dancing, and an escape from wedding world.

Diplomat. You use your diplomacy skills at work and in your family all the time, so perhaps you have the perfect solution to the steamroller-mom problem or the jealous-sister problem. When you can coach the bride with the perfect thing to say, or step in and stop bad behavior on behalf of the bride, you're single-handedly rescuing the wedding and the bride's sanity and happiness.

Network Facilitator. No, you're not setting up intricate computer systems. You're bringing all the great contacts in your own personal or business network to the bride and groom. One of the top ways brides and grooms can plan the big, beautiful weddings of their dreams is by tapping into their own and extended personal contacts to get discounts, special favors, or just suggestions on great vendors and resources. Your networking can save them thousands of dollars.

Personal Trainer. The big trend in getting fit and gorgeous for the wedding day is a healthier approach to diet and health. That counts not just for the bride but for you as well. So what better way for you all to get in shape for the wedding than by teaming up and working out together? You might sign up for a bridal boot camp class at the gym, take

Pilates classes together, even sign up for online diet and fitness programs at sites like www.shape.com and www.FitToBeTied.com. If you only have time to cheer her on, you can be a valuable part of her support system and increase her chances of reaching her fitness and health goals before the wedding.

Go-To Girl. Sometimes the bride needs a last-minute rescue. It might be going to pick up a relative at the airport when a flight is rescheduled. It might be running out to buy more ice cubes in the middle of an outdoor wedding. It might be a last-second call when the bride is sick and can't get out to pick up her rental items. In any case, you earn many gold stars (and her eternal gratitude) by doing what you can to help her out.

Glue-Gun Goddess. Here's where your crafting expertise comes into play. If you're a master of the glue gun, the diva of decoupage, or can build a chuppah out of wood and green garlands better than any designer, then your skills are a gift to the bride and groom. So much money can be saved on the wedding through do-it-yourself-ing, and the bride may not have the skills or time to make her own favors, décor, centerpieces, invitations, and programs. When you have a talent to lend, you're a godsend to the bride and groom. Some couples are so grateful, they call your contribution your wedding gift to them…saving you a few hundred dollars on items from their registry. It's a win-win!

Bodyguard. Sometimes the bride needs to be protected from people who stress her out or make her angry. It might be a lunatic relative or a bitterly jealous bridesmaid (who's about to become an ex-bridesmaid), but there are times when you just need to step in front of the upset bride and give her some space. Who knew that a helmet and shoulder pads would be needed during the wedding planning process? Sadly, it does happen that some people just push too hard, and some get downright vicious when they're not getting their way. If you can steer that angry aunt away from the bride at the shower, you can save the day.

Reality-Checker. With her emotions swirling, the wedding taking on a life of its own, and so many people coming at her from so many different directions with questions, requests, and judgments about her wedding plans, the bride can easily get swallowed up by the whirlwind. She can lose her perspective about the bigger issues—*we're getting married!*—and lock onto all the smaller details, worries, and ever-building stress from tossing one full-time job (planning the wedding) on top of her other full-time jobs (her career, family, school, parenting, etc.). It can all be too much sometimes. That's where you step in as the voice of reason and the courier of a much-needed Reality Check. It might take your sense of humor ("Hey, in a year you won't even remember the color of the ribbons on the bouquets! Don't forget...you're marrying a great guy!") or a more pointed approach ("Helllooooo! What do you care what Sarah thinks? She's not getting married, you are!"). Brides that I've spoken to have said how much they appreciated it when their bridesmaids returned them to their senses and helped them get their priorities back in line. That's what friends are for.

And of course, you may find yourself in other roles along the way: business deal negotiator, language translator at multicultural weddings, and general comic relief. Whatever your job description, whatever your role, you're a priceless part of the wedding experience for the bride and the groom.

Team-Building with Other Bridesmaids

Most important to your success as a bridesmaid—or as a Maid of Honor—is doing your part to work well as a team with all the other bridesmaids (and sometimes the moms too!). After all, you'll be planning many things together, deciding many things together, and you might all have different personal styles. You might handle tasks in different ways, which can be difficult, especially if you don't know the other bridesmaids that well, and if one or two can be...challenging. Just be responsible with what you're asked to do, be direct with other bridesmaids if you have a question or issue, ask for help or delegate tasks when you need to, and use all your social skills to keep everyone on the same team. If you have to, remind the others—in a respectful way—that this is about the bride. And do your part to make it fun!

2

A Matter of Time and Money

LET'S TACKLE MONEY FIRST...

One extra thing you'll have in common with the bride is that you're going to be pulling out your credit card...a lot. Being a bridesmaid is an honor, but it's an honor that comes with a bit of a price tag. Add up the cost of the dress (especially when the other bridesmaids agree on a pricey designer choice), the shoes, fittings, throwing a great bridal shower, your travel and lodging, and a dozen other expenses that come up along the way, and it's easy to wind up spending $1,000. And that's a conservative figure. Here's a story from a bridesmaid who perfectly illustrates the kind of financial commitment you'll likely make:

"No one particular thing cost an outrageous amount, but the expenses just kept coming! Shower invitations, the food for a shower for eighty people (the Maid of Honor went nuts), favors, a group wedding gift. At the end of it, I felt pretty awful about loading up my credit card and having to say 'No' to a vacation with other friends later that summer. I love my friend (the bride), but I really took a big hit financially to be in her bridal party."

—Kim, New York City

I'm sure every former bridesmaid in the country has a story about how her expenses grew and grew and grew. Some resent it, but others say, "It was worth every penny to be a part of the wedding, and I'd do it again in a heartbeat." Hopefully, your character is closer to the latter example and you can come to peace with the big price tags, remembering that you're doing it all as a tribute to your close relationship with the bride. Money doesn't grow on trees, but neither do the best of friends or the closest of sisters.

That doesn't mean you have to hand over a blank check and say nothing while expenses are truly getting out of control. In any bridesmaid's time, there is always a line not to be crossed. Too much may be asked of you, and the bride or the other maids might need a reminder to keep the expenses closer to earth than to the stratosphere. But how do you rein them in without looking cheap or embarrassingly strapped for cash? Simple. Don't be embarrassed, and don't worry what they think. It may look to you like all the other maids are excited about wearing Manolos to the wedding and spending $10,000 on the shower, but if you stand up and say, "Whoa, let's not go overboard," you never know, several of the other bridesmaids might be secretly relieved that you took a stand.

Here are the best ways to keep expenses down for yourself and your fellow bridesmaids:

- Don't be afraid to speak up. If that dress is out of your budget, say so.
- Come up with a beautiful alternative. If you must say no to that designer dress, have a less expensive design to suggest. You might search online for images you can send to the bride and other maids with a friendly "How about this one?" suggestion.
- See if you can barter your time for money when it comes to the shower. While many of the other maids might be able to pitch in cash-wise for a large, lavish shower, see if you can negotiate with the Maid of Honor to pitch in less money but take over favor-making, invitation-making, or other time-intensive tasks.
- Share your own cost-cutting locations, like the craft store where you know candles are much less expensive.
- Use your own seamstress if she is less expensive (and talented!) rather than following the other maids to a pricier seamstress.
- Push for non-dyed shoes. The trend for bridesmaids' shoes is moving away from dyed-to-match shoes and more toward footwear that you can wear again, like silver or gold or black, if these colors go with the dresses. Push for this option, which the other maids might appreciate as well.

When Travel Is An Issue

Of course, you know how to find great travel deals, airfares, and hotel rooms through the Internet, but you can also join in with other bridesmaids to share a hotel room or a hotel suite, book up a bed and breakfast so you can all stay together, or—even better—stay at friends' houses for the weekend. If you're able, open your *own* home to visiting bridesmaids and groomsmen to save everyone money and enjoy a festive atmosphere.

TIME IS OF THE ESSENCE

The second biggest resource you're going to be giving toward the wedding is your time. And perhaps plenty of it. Make sure that you have the time to give, and that you can manage all of the areas of your life well while you're fulfilling all your bridesmaid responsibilities.

Ideally, you'll already have considered this before you said "Yes" to being a bridesmaid—that you're not going to be on overload as you study for your finals, your bar exam, your medical exam, or as you slog through the busy season at work. We all live packed lives, and sometimes it can be hard to chisel out eight hours for sleep with everything else on our "to do" lists. As a bridesmaid, you'll need to be available for all your most important roles. Too many "Sorry, I can't make it that day" responses when the bride schedules dress shopping trips could get you fired from the job.

The top ways to make sure you have the time to devote are:

- Talk to the bride and Maid of Honor early in the process to find out which days you should absolutely block off on your calendar for any wedding plans. This means engagement parties, shopping trips, bridesmaid brunches, and especially the wedding weekend.
- Expect more than one dress shopping trip. Some brides report that they took their maids out four or five times before they found the perfect dress.
- Don't assume you'll only need the day before the wedding and the day of the wedding to be open. Brides and grooms are planning wedding weekend activities for three or four days around the wedding (such as a brunch the day after the wedding and a lineup of activities covering two days before the wedding). The rehearsal dinner might be three days before the wedding, not the night before. Be clear on what days you are expected to attend, and ask for updates so you can take time off from work.
- Allow for travel time.
- Put in for your vacation days at work as early as possible, in order to avoid hearing the boss say "No" because a dozen other coworkers already took off that Thursday and Friday.
- Let other people in your life know that you'll have Bridesmaid Duty soon. Partners, friends,

and families will then be able to give you space in your schedule.

- Check the bride and groom's wedding website frequently to catch up on any other planned activities you should or would like to attend.
- Email to confirm get-together times, parties, and shopping trip plans the day before.
- Know your own schedule. Obviously, if you know the time of the shower is likely to be a busy time for you, make all those favors, shop for all those dishware and décor items, and place your order for the menu way in advance.
- Be flexible. Schedules do change at the last moment, so do all you can to be available when you're needed.
- Be organized. Keep a detailed calendar, or use your computer's reminder system, to be sure you don't miss a fittings appointment or a pre-wedding party.

"Can I Bring a Date?"

If you're married, you definitely get to bring a date to the wedding. If you're over age eighteen or in a serious relationship, you'll *most often* get to bring a date. I say *most often* because brides and grooms are encouraged to offer the coveted "and guest" to unmarried guests as a matter of etiquette, but they may sometimes choose instead to save the open spots on their guest list for their friends and relatives. Remember, brides and grooms are under a lot of pressure to include everyone they know, and everyone their parents know. Available "slots" are prime real estate, so to speak. So don't be shocked if you don't get an "and guest" on your invitation.

If you *do* get an "and guest" as a matter of courtesy, but you're not seeing anyone seriously, you can earn your angel wings by telling the bride and groom you won't bring someone. They can then invite other guests who are important to them. It's not a huge sacrifice to give up the task of finding a rent-a-date. Going solo opens you up to the many single men who will be at the wedding and at the after party.

If you do wish to bring a guest, make sure you choose someone fun, someone social, someone you won't have to babysit all night, and someone who won't get drunk and hit on every female guest with a pulse (that includes the bride and her mom). Your guest should add to the fun without causing any fiascoes.

3

Long-Distance Bridesmaids and Other Special Circumstances

If you're concerned about how involved you can be if you live far, far away from the bride and where the wedding will take place, just relax. It may be a challenge, but it's not a problem. We live in a global society where we all move great distances for work, for love, for our interests, and we have dear friends spread all over the country and the world. It's actually *more* common now for a bride's collection of bridesmaids to be scattered than to live in the same town.

So the distance issue isn't that big of a factor, even if you're several time zones away. After all, most of the wedding plans can be made through email, instant messaging, webcam face-to-face meetings, and the occasional weekend trip to be together for dress shopping—which really isn't all that different from the usual communications used by bridesmaids who *do* live in the same city as the bride. We're all rushed and time-crunched, and we depend on emails to stay in touch. So even if you're far away, it can be very much like you're just down the street.

Making It Work When You're at a Distance

1. *Stay in contact.* Be sure you're emailing the bride or the Maid of Honor with your timely responses to any questions or plan notifications. Use your primary email account for wedding-related correspondence, not an account you only check once a week.
2. *Use receipts.* When you send an important email, be sure to click on the command that notifies you when the recipient reads your email.
3. *Is it urgent?* Click on "Urgent" for emails only when it truly is urgent and time-sensitive.
4. *Wedding websites.* Encourage the bride and groom to set up a personalized wedding website that's all about them, their wedding plans, their wedding weekend plans, easy links to the hotel, and directions to sites. This online site isn't just a great visual record of the wedding; it can be used to keep a scattered bridal party on the same page with updates, reminders, and message boards. Check out examples at www.wedstudio.com if you'd like to get a personalized wedding website for the couple as a gift (a popular choice from bridesmaids), or let the bride know about free site builders (with fewer bells and whistles) at bridal websites.

5. *Budget for travel*. You can't do the *whole* thing online, so be prepared to take two or more special trips to meet with the bride and the bridesmaids for the all-important dress shopping trip, the shower, and the wedding weekend itself. Maid of Honor, you might wish to take on the task of finding a weekend that works for all the bridesmaids to get together.

6. *Long-distance dress ordering*. Sometimes it just isn't possible for you all to get together and try on your bridesmaids' dresses in person. Time and distance may mean that you'll get an email with a link to a picture of the dress you'll be wearing, and there's no other way. So do you order the dress online and pray for the best? Well, you can, but there's a much better, safer way to go about it:

- Use that link to find out the designer name and the stores near you where that designer line is carried.
- Make some calls to see if that dress is in stock, and when you find it, take the extra time to go try on that dress style even if they only have it in another color. (Hint: some shops are crafty; they know precisely that you're coming in to try on gowns you aren't going to buy from them, so they cut the designer labels out of the sample dresses. You might have to go into the shops and look for that exact style of dress without a sales assistant helping you track it down.)
- When you can stand there in front of the mirror and say "With some alterations, I can make this work," then you'll take the next step).

- Have your measurements taken professionally by a qualified seamstress or tailor. Experts have "size cards", which are official cards where your most important measurements—bust, waist, hips, arms—are recorded by a pro. Do *not* grab a tape measure and try to take your own measurements. That's inviting dress disaster. And don't count on your regular dress size. (As in, "I'm a size 8, so order me an 8." In the world of bridesmaids' dresses, the numbers work on another scale: you might be a size 4 or a size 12 according to a designer's individual sizing rules.)
- Now here's the most important step: send in your size card to the person in charge of the entire dress order for all of you. It could be the Maid of Honor or the bride who handles the one order coming from one place, ensuring that all of the dresses are made in the same "dye lot" (in one batch) so that the colors of the dresses are uniform. Individual orders placed in different places could give you dresses in different hues, so be sure all the dresses are ordered in one place.
- Your dress, when it comes in, should be shipped to you via a company that offers registered mail, such as Federal Express. That way, if your dress is lost, they can track it down. Have it insured as well.
- You can then have it fitted by your own seamstress.

You'll find out much more about dresses in chapter seven (including *not* having to order them!), but I wanted to handle the long-distance dress ordering issue (the most stressful to bridesmaids) right off the bat.

7. *Be present in spirit.* Don't be surprised if you, even at a distance, become the Most Valuable Bridesmaid because you're *not* there: not in the bride's face, not involved in the everyday wedding planning issues and discussions (and perhaps problems). When you call or email just to say hi, you're an *escape* from the wedding world. Hearing from you is a joy when you talk about other things. That can make the bride's day.

8. *I'll be there.* Very important: Assure the bride that you *will* be in attendance, on time, at all the wedding events. She'll be stressed about so much, you don't want her losing sleep worrying about whether or not you and other long-distance bridal party members will be able to make it.

9. *Be organized.* Again, when you're far away, you need to be even more organized. Send in your updates on what you're doing for the shower and the wedding regularly and on time. Get the other maids' and Maid of Honor's email addresses and phone numbers so you all can stay in touch.

10. *Send a video greeting.* If you're in Seattle, the wedding's in New York, and the bride and groom have a large group of friends in Seattle who won't be able to make it to the wedding, you can give a priceless gift of recording a special video greeting for the couple from everyone in your long-distance group. Play it at the rehearsal dinner, at the reception, or just send it when you sense the bride needs a lift.

11. *Have a Plan B.* In case bad weather or other problems threaten your flight schedule to make it to the church on time, make sure you have a Plan B ready to go. Being there is all-important, so be ready to drive or shuffle your flights. It's worth the extra expense to be there for the bride and groom.

PREGNANT BRIDESMAIDS

What if you're going to be *very* pregnant at the time of the wedding? Of course, if your due date is the week before the wedding, you might want to bow out of the bridal party and accept another position of honor. And if your health is at risk (i.e., the doctor orders bed rest for your health and the baby's health), talk to the bride about your situation; she'll understand. Health issues aside, your biggest concern might be this: *"How am I ever going to wear a bridesmaid's dress? I'm going to look HUGE."*

Sure, it might not be fun standing next to that wispy little size 0 bridesmaid when your arms feel like sausages and you're carrying forty pounds of baby weight on you, but put those worries away! Today, pregnant bridesmaids are so prevalent in wedding parties that entire dress lines are made to suit the pregnant body! You're not huge, you're radiant! Talk with the bride about finding the perfect maternity gown. The new designer styles (as seen on celebrity moms-to-be) are just gorgeous, with beads, crystals, and necklines to show off that terrific cleavage you have now. Show off your pregnant glory and that size 0 bridesmaid will wish she looked as good as *you*. You're a walking miracle, so shine like one.

Another option for the pregnant bridesmaid is the gown with the empire waistline (think Gwyneth Paltrow in *Emma*)—so beautiful. Dress designers can suggest the perfect necklines, cuts, and even alterations (like adding illusion netting to cover your arms in a graceful and lovely way). So don't let a fear of the dress stop you or take away a moment of your excitement. Dress for comfort, including comfy shoes for the long day and night ahead.

Check with the Doctor

Of course, your health and safety come first. So check with your doctor about your travel plans (you might be advised to drive rather than fly if there's a big flu epidemic going around), and get the okay list on what you can eat and drink during the wedding festivities. You'll likely be warned against eating raw seafood, certain soft cheeses that can cause listeria (very bad for the baby!), and other questionable menu choices. As always, avoid alcohol while you're pregnant and plan to drink plenty of water and fun nonalcoholic drinks at hot-weather weddings.

Two Maids of Honor

Brides aren't limited to having only one Maid of Honor (or Matron of Honor). She might want her sister *and* her best friend standing up for her, so you might find yourself sharing the spotlight with someone else. And sometimes, that could mean mom too, as in the case of some brides choosing their mothers as their Matron of Honor and then you as the Maid of Honor. When you do find yourself as co-honor attendant, that just means you have a partner in planning, and may trade off responsibilities and expenses. The bride will decide which of you holds her bouquet during the ceremony, and which holds the ring. Other than that, it's up to you to share the role with honor and respect.

You're Having a Hard Time

If you've just been laid off from your job, gotten divorced, had a death in the family, or some other *really* difficult life passage that has knocked you for a loop, it might be tough to even think about dressing up, dancing, and smiling for the camera. You might just want to crawl under the covers.

I can't say anything to make you feel better, but I can tell you that putting on a brave face and making the most of the wedding is best for you in the long run. Not only will it lift your mood, you'll have a very happy distraction and share in the happiness of your closest friends and family. Nothing could be better for you too. Healing comes faster without additional regrets.

You're Cash-Challenged

If you're having big money problems, talk with the bride about it. She might not want you to resign from the bridal party because of a cash crisis in your life. Many brides have been known to graciously (and perhaps secretly) pay for their maids' gowns and shoes, and you can always work out a plan to contribute legwork in exchange for cash contributions.

You Have to Bow Out

Sometimes life throws us a curveball. If for some reason you absolutely can't be in the bridal party, you must let the bride know immediately. One bridesmaid from Atlanta wrote in to tell me she received her military orders to ship out with the National Guard and dreaded telling the bride. But she did tell her, and the bride understood the situation, then gave *her* a going-away party. When you truly can't serve for an unshakable reason, it's best to be direct with the bride, and offer to do something else to help out. A true friend will understand.

Part Two

Looking Fabulous on the Wedding Day

4

Your Dress

You're in luck! Today's styles of bridesmaids' gowns are a far cry from those of past decades. Designers have answered the wailing of frustrated bridesmaids and moved into the new century with gown and dress styles that are more like something you'd see on a fashion runway than on a child's birthday cake. The puffy, frou-frou, frilly, and *Gone With the Wind* styles are long gone, and now bridesmaids' dresses are stylish, sophisticated, and even sexy with plunging backs, crisscrossed halter straps, beaded bodices, sleek silhouettes, and even keyhole cutouts and bare midriffs for informal or beach weddings.

There's never been a better time, fashionwise, to be a bridesmaid. Your dress is something you can really get excited about, and you're going to look fabulous. Even better, these are dresses you'll wear again and again in the future. They're just that good.

"When Do We Start Looking for Dresses?"

For formal weddings, your shopping trip should take place six to nine months before the wedding, to give you plenty of time to shop, have your order created and shipped in, and also allow for fittings before the wedding day. If you won't be ordering your dresses, and for less formal weddings, shop according to seasonal availability, which may be three to four months before the wedding or during seasonal peak times, like when the winter formal and prom dresses come into department stores.

A Matter of Formality

Before we start talking about gown styles, we have to take care of an important factor: the formality of the wedding. As I'm sure you know, everything about the wedding plans has to fit the style and formality of the event. The bride herself has chosen her gown, train, and veil according to firm rules about lengths and styles appropriate for the time and formality of her wedding. It all has to "work." And so too is your gown bound by the rules of formality:

Very Formal Evening. Floor-length formal gown or ball gown, with elbow-length gloves.

Formal Evening. Floor-length gown, ball gown, or classy cocktail-length dress, gloves optional.

Semiformal Evening. Classy cocktail-length or street-length dress, floor-length dress okay.

Informal Evening. Street-length dress or suit dress.

Very Formal Daytime. Floor-length gown or classy cocktail-length dress; dresses are simpler and less adorned (i.e., not too sexy, not too much beading or accents).

Formal Daytime. Floor-length gown, or classy cocktail-length dress.

Semiformal Daytime. Classy cocktail-length dress or street-length dress.

Informal Daytime. Street-length dress, or even a sundress, in the case of an outdoor or garden wedding.

Bring Your Bikini

Some fun and informal beach weddings will have you and the rest of the maids in bathing suits or bikinis with color-coordinated sarongs, while the bride herself wears a white bikini with her own white sarong. From celebrities to everyday couples, this summertime beach goddess look is becoming as hot as the sunbaked sand. So don't be surprised if the bride takes you to the bathing suit section of the department store, rather than the dress section, to pick out your wedding day wardrobe!

A Matching Set or Individuals?

Here's a terrific trend that's making bridesmaids all over the country *very* happy: brides are more and more often allowing bridesmaids to choose their own individual styles of dresses, provided their choices are all the same color, length, and formality. With today's dress designers *knowing* about this trend, you'll find a range of pretty styles, all in a great color match. What this means is that you, as a group of bridesmaids, won't have to struggle to find the one design of dress that flatters *all* of you. After all, you all have different body shapes, heights, and preferences on just how much skin you'd like to show. That size 2 bridesmaid might look great in a strapless sheath, but you'd rather have a little more support up top and be a little more conservative. Now you can. You can choose your *own* bridesmaid dress in a style you *know* you'll wear again. That's so much better than shelling out $150 for a dress you look not-so-great in, feel not-so-great in, and will banish to the back of your closet.

Making the Most of Your Shape

Again, here's where you're very much like the bride. She too has looked for her gown with the goal of making her hips look smaller, or showing off those arms she's worked so hard to tone. Certain dress styles and features are ideal for minimizing certain areas and spotlighting others. Here are some general rules on which dress types make the most of your shape:

Wide Hips: An A-line dress or flared skirt is the magic touch. Avoid clingy fabrics at all costs. And sometimes it's the top that can help minimize your hips—go with a great V-neck to give you some accent up top.

Large Breasts: Look for V-necks or good coverage halter tops with a keyhole feature; avoid shirred, ruched, or cinched waists (such as an empire style), or jewel necklines that accentuate the chest. Wear a great bra for support, and then look at scoop and square necklines, without being too revealing. If all the maids are wearing strapless, you're free to ask for straps to your dress. Designers are offering new clear straps that are less obvious but still do the job well.

Small Breasts: A cinched, gathered, or ruched waist with a detailed top such as a drape-neck will make the most of your bustline; avoid strapless tops with no accent—they'll make you look smaller on top.

Plus-Sized Style: An A-line dress is most flattering, as is a high waist; nothing cinched or too form-fitting, and puffy sleeves are just a big no.

Thick-Waisted: Empire, basque, and princess waists are the most flattering; obviously, avoid corset styles, ruched, or shirred, gathered, and pinched waists that are uncomfortable.

Broad Shoulders: Go with strapless and scoop necklines, not off-the-shoulder and halter styles that bring the eye right to your shoulders.

Heavy Arms: Great sleeves to flatter arms in any shape and tone: three-quarter-length sleeves, cap sleeves, off-the-shoulder sleeves, or illusion-netting sleeves that give a wispier impression but still provide enough accent to hide any flaws.

Pregnant: Go with A-line, empire waist, and princess line, with an adjustable tie in the back.

FABRICS

The fabric of your dress has everything to do with the season of the wedding. Obviously, in winter you'll wear thicker fabrics, and in summer you'll be in lighter fabrics. Here are the most popular choices by season, although there are a wide range of fabrics that work for every season:

Spring and Summer: lightweight satin, chiffon, linens, eyelet linens, and laces.

Winter and Fall: satins, taffetas, velvets, brocades, and moires.

For every season: charmeuse, chiffon, silk shantung, georgette, illusion accents, organza, tulle, and taffeta, plus others.

Always look at fabrics for the dresses you see. It's just as important as the color of dress, because a shiny dress does accentuate your shape. Plus, in hot weather, you'll want to be sure you're in something that "breathes" and gives you more comfort.

TOPS AND BOTTOMS

You'll see a wide, wide range of gowns in terrific colors, with great accents like bead-lined bodices, plunging backs, and beaded straps. Just flip through bridal magazines for thousands of styles and visit bridal websites to view thousands more. I'd like to bring to your attention to the growing trend of bridesmaids choosing top and skirt *separates*, which allows them to choose the styles that flatter them most. We're all built differently, so mix-and-match could be the answer to your bridesmaid-dress prayers.

And *surprise*! The bride may be doing the same thing with *her* gown, using the very same designer mix-and-matched tops and skirts to create a gown ensemble that flatters her features as well.

Here are just a few samples of the kinds of tops and bottoms you'll find out there in stores, online at designers' sites, and on bridal websites:

Tops
- Strapless
- With lace paneling on the sides
- With beaded bodice
- With ruched bodice

- With embroidered bodice
- Drape (or cowl) neck
- With beaded or jeweled collar
- Halter top
- With crossed ties
- With embroidered trim
- With beaded trim
- With V-neck
- Ruched
- Brocade
- Sleeveless
- With V-back
- With illusion top
- Short sleeve with scalloped edges
- Taffeta top
- With jeweled or beaded trim
- Empire waist
- Corset top
- With lace-ups

Making Tops Extra Special

With just a well-placed accent, any top can stand out. So look at bows at the back, flattering back ties, pearl straps rather than fabric, fabric buttons in the back, and floral or jeweled pins. Illusion netting can be added as sleeves.

Jackets and Wraps

Part of your unique dress top might be a beautiful wrap or jacket worn over that sexy strapless top you've chosen. Brides request cover-ups at times when their house of worship demands no bare shoulders (sometimes a church rule) during ceremonies, and outdoor weddings could get chilly at night, so you might be asked to buy a stylish choice such as a taffeta iridescent wrap, a lace slip-on, an organza bolero jacket, or another cover-up that gives you a celebrity look: you too can enjoy an "outfit switch" by wearing the dress with the cover-up during the ceremony, and then removing the cover-up to reveal your sexy style for the reception.

Wraps and jackets might be simple, or they might be adorned with crystals, rhinestones, beads, or embroidery for an extra-special look.

Skirts

- A-lines
- Ball gowns
- Organza
- Slim full-length skirts
- Skirts with a dramatic leg slit
- Tea or cocktail length
- Taffeta
- Chiffon
- Georgette
- Satin

Skirt Surprises

Look for flowing edges that float and move when you twirl, beaded or jeweled edging at the hems, flared backs, jewel accents in a pattern at the bottom edge or back, lace-up backs and sides, and more.

STYLE NOTES

Here are a few additional style notes to be sure you're choosing the absolute best dress for you:

- An A-line skirt is flattering for most body types, so if the bride is set on having you all wear the same type of skirt, unite as a group and push for the A-line.
- If the bride is set on two-tone dresses, push for the lighter color to be at the top where it will emphasize the parts you *want* emphasized and draw attention to your face.
- If all the maids are of varying heights, be sure that cocktail-length skirts are hemmed to a uniform length from the floor, which looks better in pictures. Or, go with full-length dresses to give a uniform look.
- If the maids are of varying *ages*, select a simpler, more elegant style of dress with classic lines that looks great on everyone.
- Remember that your dresses have to look great in person and in pictures.

Gown experts tell me that softer iridescent fabrics like organza photograph well with just enough shine to them to make them look great in print. Some other fabrics like silk dupioni might be a bit too shiny.

JUST THE RIGHT COLOR

One of the biggest concerns bridesmaids all over the country (and the world) have is about the color of the dress. Will it be (gulp) peach? Purple? Fire engine red? Pale yellow?

In the best of all worlds, the bride will allow her Maid of Honor and maids to be in on the decision of dress color, but that isn't always the case. The bride may have a certain color theme in mind, and she'll just email you a picture saying "This is what it's going to be." Depending on her choice, you can cheer—or you can sink into your office chair and wonder if she's lost her mind. Hopefully, the bride will give you some say in the color choice, and she'll be open when you approach her (politely) to see if she'd consider a more sage green that will wear better than that grassy green dress she's chosen. She just might see your point and allow the switch.

Colors to Wear Again and Again

It won't take much convincing to get the bride to consider realistic colors that you'll all wear again in the future. If she's ever been a bridesmaid, she knows you're more likely to wear a red or a black dress to other events, formal dinners, dates, or the theater. This doesn't count out the top pastels. Ice blues, corals, and pinks are also on the top list of wearables that other bridesmaids say they've worn many times after the wedding.

So as a group, look beyond what would look terrific on you for the wedding day to what you'd look forward to wearing again in the future. The bride will most likely be on your side, but remember: it's her wedding. So she *can* veto your choice and stick you with the color she wants. As a good bridesmaid, it's just something you'll have to make the most of.

Maid of Honor Colors

Maid (or Matron) of Honor, you might find yourself asked to wear a slightly different color of gown than the bridesmaids. Some brides love to "set you apart" by putting you in a slightly darker or lighter color of dress, which might delight you. You might luck out and get that pretty sage green dress while all the other maids are in golf-course grassy green dresses. If you're unhappy with the color change, you can suggest to the bride that, while you love the idea of having a honored spotlight, perhaps she might do something different with your *bouquet* rather than your dress. In most cases, the bride agrees and you get to wear the prettier color.

Colors of the Season

Of course, as you know from all of fashion's rules and common sense, certain colors just work better for summer and other colors for winter.

- Spring and summer weddings are ideal for those light blues, lavenders, sage greens, buttercup yellows, soft pinks, and corals.
- Autumn and winter weddings are ideal for plums and burgundies, deep oranges, jewel tones of deep blue and emerald, and rich reds.
- Colors that work for all seasons: elegant black, coppers and silvers (lighter in spring, darker in winter), and just the right tone of red for the season.
- Seasonal colors are a judgment call on your part (and the bride's). Designers have a way of making light blue perfect for winter. It's all in the shading and the design of the dress. So check out what's showing on the market before you rule out any color.

Dress Shopping Excursions

The bride usually starts off flipping through bridal magazines or searching online bridesmaid dress collections to see which designs are a perfect fit for her wedding plans. She may sit down with all of you or with just the Maid of Honor to narrow down the choices, and then she'll come to you all (or email you) with her top three choices. At this point, you have a hand in your own dress fate.

Get in touch with the other bridesmaids (the Maid of Honor will most likely lead the way on this) to come to an agreement on which dress it will be. The best organizers of this task will ask you to rank the choices #1, #2, and #3. You may also get the option to vote "No way!" Once your votes are in, the organizer and the bride choose the final design. Bridesmaids have been known to do some campaigning to sway others' votes: "You know, it's going to be summer and we're going to be outside, so maybe that paler pink one would be better than the deep coral."

You might just bring up a good point. By no means am I encouraging you to manipulate everyone else into the dress *you* want to wear, but rather I'm encouraging you to be proactive and give yourself a better chance of wearing a dress that's better for you. It's a delicate dance at this point because the bride is being very considerate in soliciting your opinions. If it turns into warfare with three maids dead-set on the pink dress and the other three dead-set on the blue strapless, the bride's going to find herself in a stressful situation having to choose. Don't do that to her. Be agreeable, send in your votes, make your case, and hope for the best.

The Shopping Trip

Hopefully, you can all gather together in one place to embark on the dress-shopping ritual. Dress shopping might turn into two or three (or five) separate shopping days where you're pulling dozens of dresses on and off, hoping the group can reach a decision.

So many brides are allowing their maids to choose a dress of their own style choice in a matching color and this difficulty is why. If all the maids are set free to try on different tops and skirts in the same color lot, the odds are better that everyone will come to their own decisions more quickly.

Dye Lots

Very important! The colors of your dresses need to match exactly. Red can come in a range of shades, as can other colors. So it's a *must* to have all your dresses ordered from the same place, which means that they'll all be dyed in the same process with the same degree of color. Uniformity ensues, and the dresses match. When you're a distant bridesmaid, *your* dress needs to be ordered in the same batch as the other maids' so that yours matches theirs. No exceptions.

Well, almost no exceptions. Some brides are casual and informal about it, saying "Just wear your own favorite little black dress." She may want to see your dress first for her final okay, but in the case of differing shades of black, a little bit of color range is okay.

Size Cards

When it's time to place your dress order, the seamstress will measure you well and record all of your vital measurements on size cards. It's these dimensions that determine the size of dress that will be ordered for you. It's not correct to say "I'm a size 8, so get me that." Bridesmaids' gowns don't adhere to those same rules. Your dresses are ordered by dimensions, so expect that.

Distant bridesmaids, check back on page 22 in chapter three for a reminder of your special directions here!

The sales clerk will fill out detailed order forms for each of you, including all of your dimensions, the exact model number of the dress, the exact name and code number for the color you want, and any additional details. Make sure your order form is correct and that your numbers match your name on the page. Confusion on the sales clerk's part, especially when there are three Jennifers in the bridal party, can mean that you get the wrong dress.

You'll pay half of the cost as a deposit when you order the dress, and half when you receive the dress and go in for fittings. The Maid of Honor usually serves as Payment Queen, making sure you've put in your deposit and paid in full. After that, you'll all get together for fittings at the salon, if that's a part of your package, or you'll all go for fittings at a seamstress the bride has found. If you're far away, you'll find your own seamstress and be fitted perfectly for your dress.

WHEN ORDERING ISN'T NECESSARY

If the bridal party is small, and if the bride would rather not go through the hassles of ordering bridesmaids' dresses, then you might find yourselves in a great department store looking through...prom dresses? Absolutely. Today's prom dresses are stylish and sophisticated, and they can be priced very affordably. When you set off in search for your bridesmaids' dresses *at the start of prom gown shopping season* (like February or March!) you'll have a wider range of options in colors and sizes, making it possible for all four of you to find the perfect design of dress in your size.

They Can Ship It In!

If you are shopping in department stores, whether in the prom gown section or the formal dress section, know that you can ask the store sales clerk to have a dress shipped in from one of their other stores for you! Many bridal parties have gotten very frustrated that their perfect dress find was stocked in sizes perfect for four out of five brides. The fifth bride's size wasn't available. Instead of giving up and moving to another choice, ask the sales clerk to locate that size of dress at a nearby mall (they can do that!) and have it sent to their store on special hold, calling you when it arrives. Talk about customer service!

And of course, you're all free to search those department store racks to find the perfect little black (or red, or blue, or informal floral) dresses for yourselves. You'll try them on and then line up for the bride's review. Credit cards complete the purchase, and you're all set! On to the shoe department!

For Destination Weddings

If you'll be flying off to a destination wedding spot, be sure you've chosen a dress that packs well (i.e., few wrinkles) or pack it in a garment bag and bring along a steamer for last-minute touchups.

YOUR SHOES

To dye or not to dye? That is the question.

In the past, it was pretty much a given that bridesmaids' shoes would be dyed to match the dress. Now, it's not always the case.

You *may* find yourselves submitting your white satin heels in a shoebox with a swatch of your dress fabric for perfect color-matching (again, with all maids' shoes going into the same order, made from the same dye lot to ensure uniform hue). Or the bride might be on to the best new trend in bridesmaids' shoes: choosing shoes for you that don't need to be dyed.

If it is going to be a dye-job, make sure that the shoes you've chosen in the store are designated as dyeable. Some are not. And some come with instructions that they can be dyed with light-colored dyes only. Double-check on this. Some shoes' details, like rhinestone bands and lace sides, do require this special instruction.

If it's not going to be a dye-job for your shoes, then you're in luck. Many brides are making the choice to save their maids money on dyeing expenses by selecting shoes that either come in a pastel shade that works perfectly with the dress (such as pinks or light blues that are plentiful on the market) or they'll allow you to wear black shoes with your black dress. Then, there's always the stylish trend of letting you wear light *silver* or *gold* shoes, which can work with your dress and with other outfits you already own. Perfect!

Bridesmaid Shoe Design

Pretty bridesmaid shoes come in all styles and designs. The bride will most likely want you all to wear matching shoes, especially if you'll wear cocktail-length or street-length dresses where your feet will be in view. While some brides insist on matching styles, others simply say, "Wear a black shoe with an open toe." It's very important to make the distinction on open-toed vs. closed-toed, because you're all going to be standing in a line for the pictures. It's little details like that that stand out and really do matter to the bride. So if she hasn't specified open-toe vs. closed-toe, rounded-toe vs. pointy-toe (whatever's in style), make sure you ask and get the word out to the other maids (Maid of Honor, you might wish to take the lead on sending out "Shoe Alert!" emails to all the maids).

While obviously, the most important matter with shoes you're going to be wearing all day, and dancing in all night, is *comfort*. Be sure the shoe you choose is going to be comfy, with well-fitting toe boxes, straps, and any rhinestones or special accents clear of blister danger.

One valuable piece of advice if you'll be at an outdoor wedding or spending any time at all on grassy surfaces is to choose a shoe with a wider, thicker heel. This will give you more secure footing and will help you to avoid sinking into the grass as you would with thin stilettos. Thicker heels are the best choice for your own protection, and to avoid embarrassing moments—like when your shoe gets stuck in the lawn as you're walking down the aisle.

Heel height is a matter of preference and comfort. You might be happier in a two-inch heel for more secure footing and ease of dancing, or you might be used to four-inch heels. For comfort's sake, a lower heel is usually the order of the day. Never, ever agree to wear higher heels or stilettos if you're not used to them.

Shoe Styles

The bride might want you all in a very simple shoe style. After all, if your dress is detailed and accented, shoes should be simpler so as not to be "too much." But if your gown is sleek, sophisticated, relatively unadorned, and classic, you might enjoy the thrill of wearing shoes with a little bit of sparkle. Here are just some of the stylish shoe designs out there for bridesmaids:

- Satin sandals with triple rhinestone-line straps
- Strappy sandals with rhinestone floral accents
- Satin sandals with Swarovski crystal designs
- Satin sandals with crisscross straps and rhinestone baguettes
- Satin sandals with silver beads
- Lace slide sandals with beaded rosettes
- Satin sandals with lace-up ties
- Triple-strap sandals where one strap is lined with rhinestones or pastel-colored sparkles

Shoe Genius!

It's a shoe and a candy dispenser! You have to love what designers are doing with shoes these days. At the time of this writing, brides and bridesmaids by the thousands are clamoring for pretty, formal shoes where the clear, hollow heel *unscrews* so that you can fill it with beads or crystals, pearls, confetti, and even *candy*, and reattach it to the shoe. I'm not quite sure what walking around with M&Ms in your shoes would accomplish, but you have to love the ingenious way shoe designers are allowing us to personalize our shoes and make them extra-special and eye-catching. If you do fill your heels with beads, pack them tightly so they don't make a maraca sound when you walk.

ACCESSORIES

And of course, as gorgeous as you'll look in that fabulous dress and in those pretty shoes (with or without anything in the heels), there's always room for additional special touches. Here, you'll get a reminder about the top accessories to perfect your look:

The Right Undergarments. It's going to take a great bra to make the most of that strapless dress, so be sure you're shopping for the best style to suit your shape. Included in this is a reminder to keep your undergarments light-colored if your dress is light-colored. A bright blue thong will show through that pale yellow dress. A thong will prevent panty lines from showing when you have a fitted, smooth dress on, and well-fitting panties should be prechecked to make sure they're not leaving visible "squish" rolls on your hips and backside. Bodyslimmers might be on your shopping list if you like the smooth look of them (Hey, Jennifer Garner has admitted to wearing bodyslimmers when she's in formal gowns, so don't let anyone hassle you over it!)

The Best Bra

Spend time researching the best bra options to make the most of your gown appearance. For strapless dresses, consider a strapless bra if you have a moderately sized bustline, or go with a more supportive corset top. (When you're bigger on top, strapless bras can let you down in more ways than one.) For dresses with deep backlines, cutouts, or halters, look at convertible strap bras that allow you to configure your straps the best way possible. Racerback bras might work perfectly with your dress design, and you might find yourself proudly sporting a gel insert or a padded pushup bra to give more shape to yourself and your dress.

Stockings. It's a wise bride who asks her maids to wear one shade of stockings, giving you all a uniform look so that in pictures your legs all look similar shades, not too dark and not too light. Again, it's the little details that make all the difference. If you haven't been told which shade of stocking to wear, ask. As for thigh-high stockings, the new brands with rubberized "grips" at the thigh do work well, but you'll need to be sure they work well all day. At one wedding, a bridesmaid was mortified when her thigh-high stocking fell down to the floor while she was dancing.

Purses. Some brides give out pretty satin purses, perhaps with floral accents, to their maids for use on the wedding day. Pay attention to this detail, so that you're not lugging your big black purse into the reception while everyone else has pretty pink clutches.

Gloves. For formal weddings, gloves might be an official part of your wedding-day look. The bride is wearing her ivory gloves, and the maids will wear gloves to match their own dresses. It's a gorgeous formal look reminiscent of Audrey Hepburn and Grace Kelly, which is exactly why so many brides are including this choice in their ensembles.

Hats. Speaking of Audrey Hepburn and Grace Kelly, stylish, wide-brimmed, and shapely hats are back in fashion—very pretty for outdoor weddings.

The Choices in Gloves

Here's a little primer for your glove search:

- Most gloves come in One Size Fits All, so you'll want to be sure they're made of a stretchy fabric that will conform to the size of your hands, fingers, and arm. You don't want puckered, droopy gloves looking more awkward than elegant.
- Make sure gloves are designated as "dyeable" when you order them.
- Wear them just for the ceremony, and then decide as a group if you'll take them off for the reception. In some cases, when dyed gloves get wet, the color can bleed into your skin. It's also easier to eat without them on.

- Gloves come in the following lengths, which of course should be uniform for all of you: wrist-length, below-the-elbow, above-the-elbow, and opera length. Be sure when you're told to get "long gloves" exactly which length the bride requests.

Some styles you'll find out there range from elegant simplicity to adorned:

- Satin
- Matte spandex
- Shirred
- Fingerless or "gauntlet" style
- Floral lace
- Satin embroidered
- 100 percent silk
- Rhinestone-studded in an elaborate pattern, or rhinestone-studded at the edges
- And if you're looking for a bit of a fashion edge, look at the new range of wrist-length *leather* gloves that designers are showing with their bridal collections.

Jewelry. The bride might be planning to give you all matching necklaces and earrings, as her gift to you, to be worn on the wedding day for a uniform look. If you'll wear your own jewelry, check with the bride to see what style she has in mind. You might all be asked to wear something pearled, either a string of pearls or a single pearl on a pendant. Or she might ask you to wear silver necklaces and earrings. You really should have a uniform look when it comes to jewelry, and, of course, avoid wearing too many oversized pieces of jewelry. That may be your daily style, but for the wedding, matching the bride's requested look is most important.

What about That Tattoo?

You'd be surprised how often I'm asked this question by nervous brides-to-be who don't want to offend their bridesmaids. You may be proud of that tattoo on your shoulder blade, but the bride may be concerned that it won't look quite right at the wedding. She may be nervous about asking you to cover it up. This one's up to you: decide if you want to cover it with makeup, or not worry about it. The bride might be relieved if you come to her with your own question: "Would you like me to put some makeup over my butterfly tattoo, or are you fine with it?" Please don't be offended if the bride does ask you to hide the tattoo—she might be getting pressure from her mother, mother-in-law, or even her officiant over little things like that. It's not worth a fight.

5

Looking Gorgeous: Hair and Makeup

The bride isn't the only one who's going to look fabulous on the wedding day. You'll be enjoying your own share of the spotlight then and throughout the wedding weekend, so take a moment now to think about your wedding-day look: hair, makeup, skin, and a magnetic smile.

I'm not going to give you a complete primer on how to apply mascara or apply blush to make a round face appear more like Jennifer Aniston's heart-shaped face. There are plenty of magazines and beauty websites out there for that. What I *am* going to advise you on are the best tips for your best look both in person *and* in all those forever-after wedding pictures, how to deal with it when the bride has "a look" in mind for you, and how to avoid looking like a tangerine on the wedding day (and no, I don't mean wearing an orange bridesmaid's dress).

MAKEUP
Whether you do your own face or have a professional makeup artist create that "you...only better" look for

the wedding day, the key is to look as natural as possible. So many bridesmaids show up with overdone makeup that makes them look like lounge singers, justifying that they want to "show up" in the wedding pictures. With bright apple cheeks and thick eyeliner, eyebrows penciled in as dark streaks on pale skin, you're going to show up all right. Just in a very bad, laughable way. A way that will last forever in the bride's wedding photos and video. Ten years from now, the bride's precocious child will look at the pictures and say, "Mommy, who is that clown lady?" Be sure she's talking about the groom's overly painted grandmother, not you. The number one key is *don't overdo it*.

Here are the additional key cosmetic tips for your best wedding-day look:

- Apply a foundation that's close to your natural skin color. I know, you wear foundation every day, but be sure that it's a great match. We all have friends who sport "the circle" of too-dark foundation on their faces, leaving noticeable lines of color contrast on their chins and jawlines. Don't be a foundation victim. If yours is even in question, go get a color consultation at a department store cosmetics counter, or ask a friend for honest assessment of your own color.
- Wear waterproof mascara. Not just in case the tears may flow when you see the bride taking her vows; many bridesmaids have been caught in the

rain at outdoor weddings, their faces streaked with horror-show color bleeding.

- Speaking of bleeding, be sure your lipstick doesn't bleed outside the lines of your lips. Since you're going for an all-day/all-night look, apply lip liner with a lip pencil, apply a softer, more pastel or neutral shade of lipstick and then apply gloss to your lower lip for that pouty shine.
- Blush should be close to a natural shade. Going too dramatic with blush can streak you and make you look laughable. Remember, it's an accent, not a statement.
- Never wear frosted or pearlized eye shadow. Number one: it can crease in your eyelids during all-day wear, and number two: frosted eye shadow catches the light of the camera's flash and gives an eerie reflection in photos. Some bridesmaids have looked like they had light bulbs for eyeballs, and the photographer had to digitally fix the image (for extra pay) for brides who didn't want to immortalize their friends as zombie-like in their photos.
- The same goes for face powder. The camera's flash will pick up on shine, magnifying it. So be sure that you're periodically dabbing those shine lines away throughout the course of the wedding day, especially on a hot day. While makeup mavens will shout: "But being too powdered will make you look old!" (true), there's a difference between dewy and don't-y. Find the fine line

(sorry about the pun!) between applying powders and using oil blotting papers to soak up some of that shine and still leave you looking fresh.

When the Bride Wants a Uniform Makeup Look For You All

Some brides take the "you all must look alike" thing a little too seriously. I can understand wanting every one of you to have your hair in an up-do (more on that in a minute), but when a bride demands that you all wear blue eye shadow to match your dresses, that can be a problem. The bride, understandably, is trying to handle all the minor details for her wedding, and her overworked mind and overly detailed Palm Pilot can send her micromanaging your makeup. If you can live with her request, fine. "Everyone must wear neutral eye shadow" is actually a smart move on her part, to keep you all looking natural. But if you're handed a pearlized compact of sky blue eye shadow and your own applicator on the wedding day, then told to match the others perfectly, that's a bit much. Feel free to nix the blue eye shadow as a group, and agree to go neutral instead.

UP-DO OR LOOSE CURLS: YOUR WEDDING DAY HAIRSTYLE

If the bride has her heart set on you all wearing your hair up in French braids or sculpted up-do's, tucked into neat chignons or low ponytails, she's going for a uniform look that *can* be just lovely. She might request that you wear your hair loose and curly, while she sets *herself* apart from the group with a beautiful up-do, and she may ask her Maid of Honor to upsweep her hair along with her.

The great news is that hairstylists are veritable artists when it comes to up-do's. Some bridal hairstyles are just gorgeous, and you'll want extra pictures of you with your hair looking so terrific.

For finishing touches, you might be able to accent your hair in special ways, such as with jeweled barrettes or clips, a silk floral ponytail holder, or even a fresh gardenia tucked into your chignon (very stylish!). As a group, you might wear clip-in gemstone hair accents, pearl pins or tiny fresh flowers pushed into braids, or you might get to wear a colorful daisy tucked behind your ear as the perfect accent to your loose, flowing, natural hairstyle. Brides are paying special attention to these extra accents, bringing just the right touch of sparkle or decorative accent to your hairstyle.

NAILS

As bridesmaids, you might be asked by the bride to get French manicures and pedicures (if your toes will show in those open-toed shoes), again to make you all a matching group and to put the perfect finishing touch to your wedding-day look. Some brides spare their maids the expense of professional manicures and pedicures (while some *pay* for the entire group to get theirs done), and just ask that you all wear pink polish on hands and feet. This is one micromanage that's a wise move as it would be a very noticeable difference if some maids wore pink polish while others wore bright red. So don't be surprised if your nails are on the assignment list.

Be sure to ask the bride if you should have your nails done before the wedding day, or if she's planning a group trip to the salon for all of you. It's a smart move to pre-plan, so that you don't show up on the wedding morning as the only one without a mani-pedi.

THE ORANGE BRIDESMAID

Speaking of matching colors, you also don't want to show up on the wedding day with a very bad fake tan, a self-application job, or spray tan gone wrong, making you look a strange shade of tangerine or even tiger-striped with those tell-tale dark patches on your elbows, knees, and ankles. Many a bride has been brought to tears by these kinds of fiascoes, and entire teams of aunts may descend on you with lemon and salt, trying to scrub the color out of you. Don't laugh. It has happened.

If you must tan, practice with self-tanners or having tanning products professionally applied at a salon way *before* the wedding—we're talking six months here, just to be sure any splotches will fade. Obviously, watch out for tan lines from bathing suit tops. Be aware that you'll be wearing a strapless or halter dress on the wedding day, and if you do go tanning, make sure you plan your strap lines accordingly.

SKIN

Healthy, glowing skin is a must for any day, and for the wedding, you'll want to make sure your arms, legs, shoulders, hands, and face are as smooth and radiant as possible. Some brides and their maids go for facials and exfoliant treatments together months before the wedding, and some start or rev up their own existing skin care regimens with great, proven products by hydrating well and moisturizing like mad.

The One Body Part You Should Pay Extra Attention To

That would be your lips. For a dazzling smile and kissably soft lips, check into special lip exfoliant products and moisturize with terrific products like cocoa butter lip balms.

FRAGRANCE

Of course, like the bride, your idea of radiant includes wearing a great scent for the wedding day, leaving a lingering trace of you when you walk past that hot groomsman (unlike the bride, of course). My only advice on choosing a fragrance is to keep it a light scent, apply minimally, and keep in mind that many bridesmaids at *outdoor* weddings skip the fragrance so as not to attract bees and other insects that may want to pollinate with them. The choice is yours. Visit perfume counters if you wish to find a great scent for the wedding day, and perhaps a brand new signature scent of your own.

Custom Blends

Many brides and their maids are visiting specialty shops and boutiques where a trained employee will help them choose and blend completely customized scents just for them. (Are you floral? Fruity? A mix of white tea and jasmine?) This is a fun day out for all of you, if only to smell what your customized scent would be. Visit www.reflect.com as just one example of websites where you can order custom fragrances.

The key to wedding-day beauty is maximizing your strengths and being a natural beauty. And of course, your smile brings out the best of your features.

Part Three

Bridal Showers, Engagement
Parties, Bachelorette Bashes,
and Other Parties

Use the information and tips in this section for
all of the parties you'll help plan throughout
the course of the planning process.

6

Planning a Party That's Her

It's all about the bride.

Any party or get-together you plan must reflect *her* from style to theme to décor. Anyone can vacuum their living room and order five items off a caterer's list. You're going to do so much better than that. The more personalized you make it, the better. The more original, the better. The bride will forever remember the effort you put into making her party a great one.

Think about who she is and her specific style. Is she very cosmopolitan and city-chic? Then you might plan a martini party at a trendy club's private room. Is she old-style romantic? Then plan a tea at an historic home or in a garden. Is she most comfortable in a cozy, casual atmosphere? Then plan a great buffet at your place (or hers).

The most successful party captures elements of her personality and favorite things, even stepping outside the box to unique themes way outside traditional at-home parties that everyone else has had in the past:

- Wine tasting at a winery or in restaurant's private wine cellar
- Picnic at a botanical garden

- Lunch at a marina overlooking the yachts
- Elegant brunch at a five-star hotel

In this section, we'll talk about all the planning details with additional theme ideas, so start thinking now about the following:

1. What is her favorite party style? Sit-down or mingling?
2. What's her most comfortable style of dress? Casual or dress-up?
3. What is her favorite travel destination? (For example, if she loves Paris, there's your theme!)
4. What is her cultural background, and would she appreciate your giving tribute to it with a theme party?
5. What are her hobbies and interests?
6. Has she spoken about great parties she's attended in the past and loved, like a cocktail party on the roof, surrounded by lights and a view of the city? You can plan that for her.

Popular Party Themes

- Garden
- Gourmet
- Wine
- Oscar Party

- *Breakfast at Tiffany's*
- Afternoon Tea
- Paris
- Italian Countryside
- Room of the House (like the kitchen, where they both love to spend time cooking together)
- 1950s party
- USO party
- Luau
- 1980s party
- Television-show-based party, with everyone coming as their favorite TV character
- Sports theme, like baseball (everyone comes in a team jersey)
- Return to childhood
- Latin
- Mardi Gras
- Kentucky Derby
- Butterfly theme (if butterflies are the bride's fave)

COED PARTIES

Since the trend in parties for the wedding couple is moving towards His and Hers—including showers and shared bachelor's and bachelorette's parties, you'll often find yourself planning an event that's *them*. All of the ideas already suggested do apply (the guys will love a winery party too), and other popular coed party themes include winter parties and ski parties, pool and hot tub parties, casino nights, international nights, dessert and champagne parties, even golf outings.

One smart touch is to tie the theme in to the couple's history together. If they got engaged on a beach, have a beach or pool party. If a picnic was their first date, plan an elaborate picnic for them, complete with a softball game for fun. Search their history for clues, and you'll find a great way to tailor the party to them and share their story with all of their guests. It doesn't get more personalized than that.

Again, some questions to ask yourself:

1. What's their party style? Do they enjoy dressing up and going out for drinks, or are they the more laid-back types who enjoy parties at home?

2. Do they enjoy relaxed evenings, or more structured outings tailored to activities, show times, keeping a schedule?

3. What's the first thing that's popping into your mind about them? Their mutual love of the beach, a sushi party, or their love of wine and gourmet cuisine?

7

The Details

The main details you'll need to arrange for any party are:

SETTING THE DATE

Choose the best date for the party so that everyone can attend. In this hurry-up world, you might have to actually let the bride know the date of her shower. A surprise is great, but sometimes it's just too difficult to match days to the bride's schedule. Often, it's a wise move to let the bride in on the plans and give her something to look forward to.

- Engagement parties are often thrown by parents right away, but friends may also hold their own engagement parties and dinners as soon after the actual engagement as possible.
- Bridal showers take place most often 1–2 months before the wedding, but it's fine to hold this party 3–4 months before the wedding to suit everyone's schedules.
- The bachelorette's party is held most often 1–2 months before the wedding—never the night before—and sometimes only 1–2 weeks before

the wedding. Choose a date when important guests like mothers, grandmothers, and siblings can make it, and give plenty of advance notice to all guests. Especially if the event will take place during the summer, around holiday times, during spring breaks, and other busy times, the more advance notice you give, the more likely all the bride's favorite people will attend.

THE GUEST LIST

The absolute, unbreakable rule here is that you never invite someone to a bridal shower who isn't invited to the wedding. Period. If different people will hold showers in different states and invite different groups of friends, that's terrific. It's going to take some checking and organizing on the Maid of Honor's part to make sure the shower you all plan includes the right guests. Most often, you'll check with the Mother of the Bride (or the bride herself, if she's in on it) for your guest list, avoiding the dilemma of leaving someone important off the list. Flower girls are invited, along with their moms, as is anyone who's involved with the wedding.

What Happens When Mom Goes Guest-List Crazy?

I hear this one all the time. The Maid of Honor and bridesmaids are planning and paying for the shower, and Mom calls in with eighty guests she not only wants at the shower, but has already verbally invited. What to do? Maid of Honor, this one's on you. Call the Mother of the Bride and share with her your shower plans, plus the fact that your budget allows only for a smaller group. Let her know that she is welcome to help pay for the guests she's invited, otherwise—and this is where you have some bargaining power—you're going to have to plan a much less formal, casual party instead of the lovelier, more formal one she has in mind. Mom should offer to help out.

For the bachelorette's party, ask the bride who she wants to come along. The guest list will most often include all of the bridesmaids, the bride's close friends, perhaps coworkers and cousins. Even some moms and aunts have joined in for the earlier stages of the party. If the bride makes up her list, you don't have to worry about leaving someone important out.

LOCATION
Find a great place with a private room (very important!), great atmosphere, and perhaps even a unique twist...like a restaurant overlooking the beach, or a garden terrace for dining al fresco. If the party will be held at a private home, make sure you all pitch in to help clean and set it up (that means cleanup duty as well), and most important, that there is more than enough seating for everyone and space to move around. Jamming fifty people into a tiny apartment

where they're sitting on the floor during two hours of gift opening makes your party a disaster. When scouting for locations, check with the other bridesmaids or family friends to see if anyone is a member of a private club or country club, an alumni club, or association with a clubhouse where you might gain access to a great setting for a discount.

REGISTRY ETIQUETTE

How do you let guests know where the bride is registered when etiquette states you're not allowed to mention anything about gifts on any invitations? Well, today's grasp on etiquette is loosening a little bit, and many bridesmaids choose to forego the old propriety rules and just write down the bride's registry information on shower invitations. The guests, after all, want to know, and it's just easier. Very often, and for those who *do* wish to follow etiquette, the solution is to provide the bride and groom's personalized wedding website, telling guests that all registry and wedding information can be found at www.___. Problem solved, and you've still led everyone right to their registry link. Otherwise, the couple's registry details are shared by word-of-mouth.

INVITATIONS

There's no need to order expensive professional invitations or spend hours hand-writing those fill-in-the-blanks invitations from the card store. It's much easier and more efficient to get blank invitation cards or decorative paper from an office supply store (see Resources) and create your own invitations with colored print, playful fonts, and even graphics from your own digital camera.

Choose a theme design that fits the event and the bride's personality, and get creative with it. You might even copy formal wedding invitation styles by punching a hole at the top of the invitation card and tying it with a color-coordinated ribbon bow. Or use a theme-shaped hole punch (very inexpensive from the craft store) to pop some hearts, cherubs, or shooting stars into colored invitation card stock for the only decoration you'll need. Some bridesmaids pull out their rubber stamps and colored ink, embossing powders, even wax seals to make their invitations *look* professionally-done, but for far less.

Emailed invitations (such as through www.evite.com) are fine for informal get-togethers like bridal brunches and for the bachelorette's party (you can keep easy track of RSVPs through those online services) but for the shower, stick with printed and mailed invitations. Some guests might not have access to email, as has been reported by many grandmothers and great-aunts in the past few years. Set an early RSVP date with your phone number and email, and keep careful track of your responses so you can plan your party perfectly.

Who is This Party For?

I've received bridal shower and bachelorette party invitations and had no idea who they were for. They just said "Jennifer's Bridal Shower." I know about twelve Jennifers, four of whom were planning weddings that season. Keep this is mind: people on your guest list may be from the groom's side, or they too might have a dozen Jennifers getting married soon. So always put the bride's full name (and the groom's, if it's a coed party) on your invitations just to be safe.

DECORATING

The most exciting thing is that you don't need to go wild with decorating to make an impact. In fact, less is more when it comes to decorating for parties. Simple elegance or understated playful accents always make more of an impression on the bride and on the guests. With a few well-chosen décor ideas, you can set the perfect stage for the party.

- First, see what you already have. Use your own fine china set, or ask a friend to bring hers over to mix with yours. Borrow a punch bowl and serving platters. Use your own pillar candles from your bedroom. Don't go shopping until you, as a group, have discussed what you can bring to the party from your own supplies.
- For flowers, you can get one beautiful over-sized floral arrangement for the entryway, and

then center your tables with adorable $5 potted gerbera daisies from the supermarket. These potted flowers can be take-home prizes for your games, too.

- Color-coordinate for a theme party. At one recent bridal party where the bride's colors were pink and brown, the bridesmaids placed bowls of inexpensive pink and brown candies on each table, on countertops, on windowsills and then set out pink votive candles or single pink flowers in bud vases. A perfectly designed color scheme was born—including a pink-frosted cake.
- Purchase color or theme-matching plates, cups, and utensils from a party supply store and build your theme while you make cleanup incredibly easy later.
- There's no need to decorate the buffet table. While you could add a few of those $5 gerbera daisy plants between serving platters, it's not a necessity when the food is attractive.
- Share a frequent wedding décor idea by setting up a table filled with fun framed photos of the bride (and groom, if possible). Put out a guest signing book, and your décor is a conversation starter too.

Pictures from the Process

Forward-thinking bridesmaids have taken fun pictures of the bride throughout the planning process—such as at her engagement party, during dress-shopping trips, during cake-tasting trips, at wine tastings, and visits to relatives, etc.—and then set out *these* pictures of the bride at the shower, together with explanations of what was going on, and what the bride was thinking.

And of course, for bridal showers, don't forget about the wishing well. In some regions of the country, it's tradition for the bridal shower hosts to set up a wishing well (easily made, rented, or borrowed) where guests are to place very inexpensive household items. With the words "Wishing Well" printed on your invitation, guests know to bring along such items as spices, dish towels, barbecue sauces, measuring spoons, paper plates, and other household goods the couple will use in the future. Some Maids of Honor and bridesmaids invite shower guests to print up their favorite recipes on index cards and drop those into the wishing well also. If you can't locate a mock wishing well, get creative. Some bridal parties have used little red wagons, suitcases, and large decorated boxes with the words "Imagine This is a Wishing Well" on it.

MENU

A terrific party calls for a terrific menu, so make it unique and tasty, and of course, tailor it to the personalities and favorites of the bride and groom.

The food makes the party, so if you're in charge of the choices, keep a few things in mind:

- Whatever you supply, it has to be *good*. Never prepare food items you haven't personally tasted first. If you're using a caterer, ask for a tasting before you order.
- Sometimes you wouldn't dream of hiring someone to make the food, or even buying frozen appetizers to heat up and serve. You have access to the bride's mother or father, grandmother, or a special aunt whose famous dishes will make the bride's day. It's incredibly popular to have Mom make her apple cobbler or her lasagna for the party, and as that's the bride and groom's favorite dish, including it is a win-win.
- Or, do as so many other bridal parties have done and get together a few hours before the party and prepare the meal and snacks yourselves. With you all gathered together, talking as you cook, the party preparations become another great group activity—and you should know that many grooms and groomsmen, fathers and grandfathers are all too happy to join in to make their garlic bread, antipasto, bruschetta, or chocolate cream pies. Many bridal parties say the food prep time was the most fun they've had in a long time.
- Be sure to select unique menu options in addition to crowd favorites. You don't want the same

menu everyone has at their parties. So go with the lemon chicken and the ziti, but add in a Moroccan bean salad or spring rolls for something new and exciting.

- Go with theme menus when you can, including international themes. Be sure all your choices work together.
- Include some non-meat food choices for guests who are vegetarian, some vegan options, or whatever matches your guests' tastes.
- Include seasonal specialties like a baked ham during winter holiday months, or seafood that's in season.
- Think about letting guests make their own food. No, not handing them a skillet and some eggs, but rather laying out the makings for their own panini sandwiches or crepes and letting them personalize their own dishes. The same works with fondue sets or a pasta bar, even a make-your-own burger bar.
- Include kid-friendly choices on the menu if the little ones are invited to the party. Some chicken fingers and mini pizzas might be ideal if everyone else is eating spicy Thai food.
- Include some healthier choices, like fruit platters or healthy salads that are not made with creamy sauces. Guests on health plans will appreciate your forethought.
- Label foods that are unique, such as printing out cards that specify beef empañadas or vegetable

spring rolls. Guests who don't know what's inside wrapped items may not be likely to indulge.

- Recreate the menu of the couple's first date. If they went out for Cajun food, make it a Cajun party with crawfish, jambalaya, jalapeño cornbread, and ribs.

- For breakfast and brunch parties, get creative with "the usuals." Add in eggs benedict or really unique bagel spreads like cream cheese mixed with caviar, herbs, hot peppers, or salmon. Use unique fruits in fruit platters like mangoes, kiwi, and starfruit instead of plain cantaloupe. At a hotel's brunch, you'll probably find breakfast foods (scrambled eggs, bacon, sausage), seafood bisques, prime rib carving stations, and a dessert buffet you'll want to stop at *first*. This alone is one reason why brunch parties at hotels and restaurants are picking up speed as *the* top choice for wedding-related parties.

Desserts

The sweetest part of your menu could be a mini wedding cake or a standard sheet cake. Creative party planners tell me they're going to bakeries and even ice cream shops to have specialty cakes made with pictures of the bride and groom printed or airbrushed on top. A great big sheet cake with a terrific, unique filling always pleases the crowd, as do cupcakes for a unique spin on the traditional cake idea. If you'll have a desserts-only party (as is another growing trend), choose delicious mousses, pastries, fruit tarts, cobblers, cakes, pies, and even tortes. Add in bowls of fresh fruit with whipped cream, or chocolate-dipped strawberries. Check out alternatives on chocolate-dipped fruit, since you can find white-chocolate-dipped berries rolled in mini chocolate chips, plus other unique choices like caramel dips and almond-flavored dips. Chocolate truffles, chocolate covered candies, and even snack favorites like Twinkies end the party with a very happy sweet tooth.

DRINKS

For any party, make sure you're choosing quality wines and champagnes that you've tasted, or vintage favorites of your own. Check out the best newly rated vintages on the market by searching www.winespectator.com, where you'll find recommendations in several price brackets. Consider sprucing up champagne with orange juice for mimosas, or with fruit juices for a bit of color. For mixed drinks, look at martinis and mojitos, Bay Breezes and cosmopolitans. Soft drink lovers will appreciate great, unique choices they don't get every day: orange soda (to match the color scheme), birch beer, cream soda, or iced teas and lemonades with a twist. To finish off, provide great quality coffees and flavored teas, and in winter don't forget about great hot chocolates (including hot white chocolate), eggnogs, spiced ciders, and hot toddies. Add playful drink stirrers to terrific glasses for a stylish serving.

FAVORS

At any party where guests will take away a favor, make sure it's something they can use. Going unique is the biggest challenge for party hosts, as many bridesmaids report in that they want to give something, *anything*, other than a little silver picture frame. The most popular (and also the most inexpensive) choices are:

- Boxed chocolates or tulle bags of colorful candies (jelly beans, Skittles, or even personalized color blends of M&Ms that you can order directly from the M&Ms' website: www.mms.com)
- Gift books and quotation books
- Journals
- Photo albums
- Music CDs
- Candles
- Bath salts or bath oils
- Beauty specialty products like fragrant exfoliant scrub salts with a loofah
- Perfume sprays
- Perfume compacts
- Lip gloss trios
- Wine charms
- Herb plant seedlings in pretty pots with a ribbon bow
- Fuzzy slippers
- Toys or something more playful that fits the bride's personality (perhaps toy tiaras—always fun to put on when you're in a bad mood or when

slogging through endless paperwork on the week-
ends—Magic 8 balls or their pink counterparts
the Magic Date Ball, Mad Libs, and so on...)

Each of these items also have prize potential,
meaning you can give them away as prizes for the
winner of each shower game. For additional prizes
in the bigger-ticket category, look at gift certificates
to dinner, the movies, beauty salons, wine shops,
home décor stores, and bookstores; kitchen garden
plants or potted flowers, a spa robe and slippers, or
a basket of beach-read novels.

GAMES

You can certainly plan to do the shower games you've
seen at many, many showers before yours (like the
clothespin game where you'll take a clothespin from
the guest who broke "the rule" and crossed her leg,
touched her face, or said "hello"—whatever's been
designated as the game hinge) and give it a fun new
twist (like replacing that clothespin with a crystal
bead bracelet you've bought in bulk from a party
supply or craft store). Other party games:

- A trivia game you've created with questions
  about the bride and groom
- Bridal bingo, where you'll print out blank grids,
  and guests will fill each square with a gift they're
  sure the bride will receive. As the bride opens
  her gifts, guests play along and circle the items

they've written down. First one to get Bingo gets a prize, and onward until three to five prizes are awarded. The Bingo grid may look like this:

	B	I	N	G	O
B	Blender	Coffeemaker	Toaster	Waffle iron	Silver platter
I	Bedsheets	Washcloths	Towels	Water glasses	Wine glasses
N	Measuring cups	Spatulas	Egg timer	Espresso cups	Tablecloth
G	Cutlery	Saucepan	Candlesticks	Duvet cover	Wire whisk
O	Pillows	Blanket	Water filter	Gravy boat	Salt shaker

- A concentration game where many household items are shown, several are taken away, and guests have to guess which ones are gone.
- A word scramble where guests have to see how many words they can make from the letters of the bride and groom's first names.
- Pop culture trivia games, including those with DVD graphics and video clips.
- Asking guests to write down what the couple's first dance song should be and why (you'll get some funny answers!).
- Create a twist on old college drinking games. Without the bride knowing, designate several

things she might say that indicate all guests must lift their glasses, say "Cheers!" and drink to her. After a short time, let her in on the game so it doesn't get annoying.

- Create a toast game. Each player draws a card, and then using the prompt on the card, he or she must propose a toast in the manner described—such as "Propose a toast in an English accent," "Propose a toast in a different language," "Propose a toast in which every sentence is a question," "Propose a toast where you will say 'ya' know?' after each sentence," and "Propose a toast as an imitation of (a celebrity)." Get creative with these cards, and be sure to catch it all on video.

- The bride and groom timeline game. On a corkboard with pushpins, your guests will arrange cards printed with calendar dates to match the event in the couple's history that took place on that date. For instance:

May 25, 2001: Bride and groom's first email contact

May 26, 2001: Bride and groom's first phone conversation

May 30, 2001: Bride and groom's first date

May 31, 2001: Bride and groom's first kiss

June 2, 2001: Groom sends roses to bride at work

June 8, 2001: Bride tells mother that groom is The One

June 15, 2001: Bride and groom's first weekend trip

July 12, 2001: Groom tells his buddy that the bride is The One

September 12, 2001: Bride meets the groom's parents

September 18, 2001: Groom meets the bride's parents

December 24, 2001: Bride and groom get engaged (and so on...)

Especially at coed parties, this one is fun when you separate the women and men to let them each see if they can figure out the timeline (the bride and groom do not participate, so that they don't get in a fight when the groom—or the bride—gets the engagement date wrong!). You keep the master list, and the winning team gets the prize.

Toasts

Speaking of toasts, when you make yours, find the right mix of humor and sentiment, always adding great stories of your history together and wishing the couple well. Talk about your memories from when the bride and groom first met, what she may have said after their first date, when you knew he was The One for her, and how she's changed for the better since meeting him. Be sure to let the moms know they're welcome to give toasts too, even if they're not hosting the party, and let the bride take the floor to say a few words of her own.

Bridesmaid Duty

At the bridal shower, as the bridesmaid or the Maid of Honor, you may be assigned to create a faux bouquet from the bows and ribbons off the gift boxes. When there are far too many bows for one bouquet, you can make a hat out of the second paper plate base.

You also might be asked to write down every word the bride says (as the traditional game of what the bride or the groom will say on the wedding night), or keep an organized written record of who gave which gift to the bride and groom for thank-you purposes later.

BRING IN THE EXPERTS

At some bridal showers, bachelorette parties, and even post-dress-shopping dinners, you might wish to make the party extra special by hiring a professional to come in and serve your group. No, not that kind of professional! I'm talking about manicurists; massage therapists who can do your necks, feet, or hands; or astrologers; henna artists; caricature artists; and any other fun entertainer you can find. One bridal party reported that they found firemen who double as sexy balloon artists. I don't know how they found them, but people are still talking about the hot, shirtless firefighter balloon artists. I'm thinking of inviting them in for my birthday party.

SHOWERS YOU'LL ATTEND, NOT PLAN

Brides are often given *lots* of parties, perhaps even up to five individual showers thrown by her friends, her work friends, people in her hometown, people in the groom's hometown, and so on. Lucky her! As a bridesmaid, you're often considered a must for each guest list, and you really should go to all the parties you're able to attend. Do you have to bring a big gift to each party? You should bring something to each, but don't worry about splurging on expensive gifts for five different parties. Just give the bride something great at one (perhaps the one you're throwing for her) and then bring a little extra something to other parties you attend. You should never attend empty-handed and state that you already gave her something previously. Even if it's just a pretty candle set, bring a gift.

8

Bachelorette Party Specials

For "Girls' Night Out," the level of wildness is going to depend on the bride's wishes and personality. She may be the type to enjoy a night of drinking, male dancers with bottles of Hershey's syrup and a blindfold, and craziness to rival even the most out-of-control bachelor party some guys have. Or she might prefer to skip the shots and the male dancers in favor of something more serene—like a weekend at a spa with the girls.

The current styles of bachelorette parties swing between both extremes.

For the wild night of partying, you might rent a limousine or a party bus (safety first, always!) to take you from club to club to club (to club to club), or you might bring the festivities to your own home, opening up your doors to a pair of deliciously hot "police officers" (wink, wink) and mixing drinks at your own kitchen counter.

For the wild party, it's up to all of you to decide just how wild it will get. Will you have one male dancer or three? Just how raunchy do you want the gifts to be? As mentioned earlier, many brides-maids and brides report that their parties were slightly out of control, and many hangovers were apparent the next day. Your job as a bridesmaid, or as the Maid of Honor, is to watch out for the bride. If she's drinking a lot, keep her out of trouble— especially trouble she may not remember the next day, but could regret for the rest of her life. If you know she doesn't drink a lot, make sure others aren't pushing drinks or shots on her, and give her the easy out by removing her from a situation that has clearly gotten out of your and anyone else's control due to the influence of other people who've joined your party, or other bridesmaids or friends who have some serious rehab in their futures.

Save the Bride!

When you're out at the club, be sure you rescue the bride from any too-friendly guys on the dance floor or at the bar. You know how to pull a friend from the clutches of Mr. Smooth or Mr. Gold Chain and Chest Hair. Some bridesmaids physically pull the bride away from the guy on the dance floor, or very deftly dance their way between the bride and the touchy-feely predator who's moving in too close.

The bride may wear a tiara and veil to make her stand out, or she might wear an "I'm the Bride" tee shirt or other slogan tee shirt, and you might charge her with the task of having to dance with the good-natured bartender. She can look, but not touch, after all! And if *you* want a bit of extra attention too, you all might wear matching tee shirts or tank tops that announce you as Bridesmaids. Watch how many times you get asked to dance!

Watch Your Wallet!

Worried about what it will cost for your twenty female friends to have dinner out and then drink for six hours after dinner? In some cities, drinks can be $10 *each*! How do you swing the bachelorette's party without going broke, and without visibly stressing over how big that bar tab is growing? Limit the cash bleeding by having dinner and a round of drinks at home first, where you can supply a budget-friendly but still fabulous meal and great drinks for far less than at a trendy restaurant or bar. *Then* you can all hit the town and party without worries.

Elegant Nights Out

You may call it a Bachelorette's Party, but it has nothing in common with the wild packs of drunken revelers passing you on the street on the way to the nearest college bar. These parties include a great night out at a jazz club, tickets to the theater or a play, or a terrific five-star dinner at a top restaurant with the best wine and desserts you've ever had. Some groups go to special presentations at museums or aquariums, or even art gallery openings—the perfect match of cultural style to the bride's tastes.

Hitting the Road

Another big trend in bachelorette parties is taking a road trip. The girls may all fly out to Vegas for the weekend for three days of celebrations, testing your luck at the roulette table, taking in shows and free buffets, and enjoying resort amenities. You might take a trip to the beach, or go to a spa for the weekend for the full royal treatment. Some brides and maids head out to wine country for bike tours, wine tastings, antiquing, and food tours. Others reserve a terrific bed and breakfast for a relaxing weekend all together. Some go to a nearby hotel for dinners, spa treatments, use of the pool and hot tub, brunches, and full, uninterrupted days laying out in the sun. Ask the bride which style of road trip she *has time for* before you book anything. Especially in the weeks before the wedding, she may have a packed schedule.

Active Event

This idea works for coed parties as well, and a growing number of party groups are choosing to do something active, like rock wall climbing, hiking, scuba diving, canoeing, kayaking, whitewater rafting, horseback riding, or even going to amusement parks.

Giving Gifts

At the bachelorette party, there's no need for you all to bring individual wrapped gifts. Just arrange for everyone to go in on a group gift: like a day at the beauty salon or a massage when the bride returns home from her honeymoon. Also welcome: gift certificates for dinners out, or show or concert tickets.

Joining With the Men

Some brides and grooms would be much happier with a *shared* event: a Bachelor-Bachelorette's Party. Sure, there may be some element of "I want to keep an eye on him/her," but usually it's just that the entire group gets along so well that they'd rather spend time together than split into two groups. It's just more fun that way.

If you're planning a coed bachelor-bachelorette's party, you have terrific options open to you. You might do the group pub crawl thing, hitting every hot dance club in town for a wild night that lasts until 4 a.m., or you might do as so many others have done and plan an event like the following:

- Tickets for all to a major-league or minor-league ball game. You can get box seats, have it catered, get cigars for the guys (and the women who partake), have great wines and drinks served by your own bartender, or sit in the bleachers for hot dogs and cold beers.
- A trip to a winery is a great day out for all.
- Plan a weekend at a shore house, taking in the relaxing summer scene, holding clambakes on the beach, and doing group activities like taking dinner cruises or going jet-skiing.

- Try some of the same active events as previously listed: rafting, kayaking, horseback riding, amusement parks, etc.
- Have a ski weekend at a great lodge where those who ski can do so, and those who wish to hit the hot tub can do so as well. Grab drinks at the ski lodge and dinner at a great restaurant. Then, head out for sledding, nighttime ice skating, or a sleigh ride.
- Take a dinner cruise around the city harbor.
- Get group tickets to a great concert or show, either box or lawn seats—whatever works for your group's budget.
- Go to a comedy club and make sure the comedian knows there's a bride and groom sitting right there, ready to be part of the act.
- Host a terrific homemade sit-down dinner at your place with great wines and great conversation, perhaps even a movie night.

9

Bridal Brunches, Coffees, and Meetings For Martinis

This section is just to remind you to make plans with the bride and the other bridesmaids not only for planning sessions, but also to relax and de-stress, laugh and gossip, catch up on the latest reality shows, and give the bride something she really needs—a break from wedding world. She needs quality time with her women friends to keep some semblance of her pre-engaged life intact and remind herself that she is a person beyond being a bride.

- Bridal brunches are traditionally planning meetings for the group, but you can designate the first half for wedding talk and the second half as "no wedding talk allowed!"
- Making plans to meet for drinks on Friday nights after work could be ideal, but if the bride's schedule is jammed, make it a set plan to meet every *other* Friday night. She'll look forward to each stress-free outing.
- Ask the bride out for coffee every once in a while. As many brides have told me, "I hate it

that no one calls me except when they need something for the wedding, or they have a question about the wedding. I need a break!" Be that break she needs and just ask her out for a quick cup of coffee or for breakfast.

· Another ritual you might create is meeting at a bakery to grab a mini pastry and a coffee or cappuccino.
· Or just meet at the park for a sandwich lunch, a soda, and a long walk during your lunch hour.

These meetings allow you to be the friend you've always been, keep the dynamic of your friendship alive, and—as many brides have confessed—keep the bride sane and de-stressed so that she doesn't snap at the groom or her own mother. With this ten-minute meeting or long lunch, she has enough of a decompression and recharge to be able to *enjoy* her wedding planning process. So make that call and ask her out for coffee. Set up that happy hour. Make sure all planning meetings include plenty of laughter.

Part Four
About the Wedding
Ceremony

10

Ceremony Etiquette

Just a few rules of etiquette for during the ceremony itself:

1. Smile at all times, especially when walking down the aisle.

2. Be aware that *everything* is caught on videotape. Countless brides have watched their videos in horror when they see one bridesmaid in the background rolling her eyes or mouthing words to her boyfriend in the seating area the whole time.

3. Know your responsibilities and keep them sacred. Maid of Honor, you must have the groom's ring in hand, and you must know how and when to arrange the bride's train so that she can move gracefully. If you must step forward during the ceremony to fix a tangled train for optimum beauty as photos are being taken, you may do just that. Guests understand, and the couple will thank you later.

4. Know the time and place for jokes. Sure, you might think it's funny to hold up signs rating the

bride and groom's first married kiss as a 10, 9.5, or 6.5, but relatives might dislike you for it.

5. If you feel faint, step aside and sit down. Don't try to tough it out, or you could fall face-first.

6. Top tips to prevent fainting: don't lock your knees while you're standing, breathe slowly and deeply, and be sure you're hydrated.

7. Make sure you meet the bride's eyes if you can. Giving her a little wink is a great moment.

8. Respect all religious and cultural traditions. If the bride and groom have some—shall we say—*interesting* spiritual elements in their ceremony, show no judgment. It makes them happy.

The Best Wedding Gift

As a bridesmaid, your greatest gift is your participation in the wedding day itself. But you'll also need to give not just one, but *several* additional gifts to the couple. We're talking an engagement gift, shower gift(s), and a wedding gift.

As a Matter of Etiquette...

Etiquette says you have up to a year to deliver a wedding gift to the bride and groom. Even with that rule in place, it's always best to bring a gift with you, so that the couple can open it in your presence.

Of course, you know the bride and what she's most likely to receive. Picking a present for her is going to be a snap. But as part of the bridesmaid group, you'll often have the choice of giving an individual gift *or* giving a larger group gift from all of you. Most bridesmaids groups do choose to give a bigger present from themselves as a group gift, so check out the following tips:

1. Decide if you really want to give an individual gift, and let the Maid of Honor know in advance so that you're not pressured into chipping in more than you can spare for a group-decision massive gift.

2. Make great use of the bride and groom's bridal registry, and order your gifts early while the more affordable presents are still available on the list.

3. Consider giving the bride and groom not a wrapped gift, but an *experience,* such as his and hers massages before the wedding or a champagne dinner cruise during their honeymoon. Experience gifts make lasting memories.

4. Another experience you can give them is a pair of tickets to a concert or show they've been wanting to see. Especially if the event takes place before the wedding, you've given them a great night out together, a great stress-reliever for the bride, and another terrific lasting memory.

5. For personal gifts to the bride, such as for her bachelorette party or as a shower gift, go with something sentimental, like a framed photo of the two of you as little girls, a scrapbook you've made of your favorite memories (the entire group of bridesmaids can make this together, too!), or mixed music CDs with all your favorite songs. These sentimental choices can also be add-ons, separate little gifts given in addition to the larger group gift.

6. If the bride and groom have everything they could ever need (as some couples do) and they believe strongly in a charitable cause, make a donation in their names and give them a card stating that fact.

Great Group Gifts

Here are some of the most popular group gifts bridesmaids give the bride or the couple:

- Place settings of their china pattern
- Settings of their crystal stemware
- Bed linen ensembles, especially if they're luxurious, such as 100 percent Egyptian cotton sheet sets or cashmere
- A hammock
- Food processor/mixer sets
- A complete set of their cooking pans
- A complete set of their casual dinnerware

And of course, you might also follow in the footsteps of other bridal parties who give the couple something they can *really* use, like home cleaning services for a year, landscaping services for a year, membership to a health or tennis club, personal chef service for a year—something that will really enhance their life together.

Whatever you choose, remember that presentation is important. So don't just dump the present into a pink gift bag. Make it special. Choose some of the decorative, creative wrapping envelopes and boxes that are out on the market today.

12

The Rehearsal and Rehearsal Dinner

Practice makes perfect, and since the bride and groom want everything to go as perfectly as possible on the wedding day, the rehearsal is serious business.

Don't Miss It!

For scheduling purposes, keep in mind that everyone's busy schedules *might* mean that the rehearsal and rehearsal dinner could be planned for several nights before the wedding, not just the night before. So make it a point to check in with the bride if you'll have to travel to attend the wedding.

Dress for the rehearsal dinner is often casual-nice, a pantsuit or a dress. This isn't a time for jeans and a tee shirt, since the rehearsal dinner afterwards could be planned as a fairly formal or semi-formal affair. The hosts will let you know. Show up on time, if not early, and be ready to listen.

The officiant and the wedding coordinator will most likely lead the show, letting you all know how to line up, when and how to walk down the aisle, and where to stand or sit. Maid of Honor, you'll be instructed on when to step forward to take the bride's bouquet and hand her the ring. During this run-through, everyone learns the order in which the ceremony events will take place, and, especially if there will be unique cultural elements and rituals in the ceremony, what exactly will take place when. Those who will perform readings or musical performances will do a run-through as well, and the bride and groom may practice their vows and kiss.

When it comes to the formal rituals of the ceremony itself, don't be afraid to ask questions. If, for instance, the ceremony is going to be a high Catholic mass and you're not Catholic, what do you do if you don't wish to receive communion? At one wedding I attended, a bridesmaid caused more than a stir (it was an outrage to religious guests) by accepting the communion wafer from the priest, and since she didn't know what to do, *stuck it in her bouquet*. Talk about a *faux pas*! Some guests expected her to get struck by lightning right there on the spot. So don't be afraid to speak up. The officiant will guide you. The same goes with asking the officiant to give you directions on when to sit and stand.

You'll practice filing back down the aisle for the recessional, and even do a practice lineup for the receiving line. There may be two or three run-throughs, lots of questions, and perhaps a few delays for flower girl and ring bearer instruction.

Once complete, the rehearsal gives you all the relief of knowing what to expect, and makes the impending wedding day all the more real for the bride and groom.

THE REHEARSAL DINNER

Once the rehearsal is done, it's time for you all to head to the rehearsal dinner, where you'll enjoy the excitement and share plenty of hugs with the bride and groom in a relaxed atmosphere with great food and wine (or a great barbecue and beer!). The key to a terrific rehearsal dinner is making plenty of toasts. The couple will toast their parents and *you* for helping to create their big day, they'll toast each other, the parents will propose toasts to their kids and the future in-laws, and *you* too may choose to lift your drink and say a few words of praise and congratulations to the bride and groom. At this event, perhaps even more so than at the reception, it's a close, intimate group, so the toasts are funny, sentimental, and filled with emotion. This could be where the best toasts take place, giving the bride and groom a wonderful sense of being fully loved by all their most favorite people right there in one room.

Gifts are exchanged, perhaps with presentations to each member of the bridal party, and then it's your turn as a group to give the bride and groom their wedding gift. This would be a great time to let them (and everyone else) know that you booked them a special treat—swimming with dolphins at the honeymoon resort—something you know the bride has always wanted to do. Make your presentation special, and no one will ever forget how terrific you are and how perfect your gift is for the couple.

Finally, make sure that if the wedding will take place the next day, you don't get too drunk (as some bridesmaids have done in the past, showing up for the wedding late or hung over), and that you share some quiet time with the bride before you all head home for the night.

13

The Wedding Morning

When you show up at the bride's place ready to mobilize for the excitement ahead, here are the top tips and to do's on your list as the ideal bridesmaid:

- Show up on time, ready to go, with everything you need in tow.
- Help set up the bridal breakfast, a buffet so that everyone can help themselves: bagels and cream cheese, pancakes, a bowl of berries or sliced melon, the works... It's important for everyone to get food in their stomachs and energy for the big day. If you're the Maid of Honor, show up early to help set up the bridal breakfast and just hang out with the bride over coffee during the last few quiet moments she will have all day.
- Bring a wedding-morning gift for the bride and her family: flowers in a vase, some extra breakfast treat like pastries, a bowl of berries, a bottle of champagne for a toast or mimosas, etc.
- You might be a courier for the groom, bringing the bride a card, flowers, or a gift from him as a surprise.

- Attend the salon visit with the bride and have your hair, nails, and makeup done. If the bride has salon professionals coming to your site, help keep the flow of primping bridesmaids running smoothly so that everyone is "done" on time.

- Get dressed, and then help the bride get dressed. As a helpful hint to you all, be very, very sure your dresses are pulled on with extra care taken to prevent your lipstick or makeup from getting on them. Some brides have teams of bridesmaids holding the neckline of the dress far away from her face while she shimmies into it and gets it zipped up, and others actually cover the bride's face with a *pillowcase* when extra care must be taken to keep lipstick marks and foundation away from the white dress.

- Maid of Honor, it's your duty to make sure everyone gets the correct bouquets, corsages, and boutonnieres from the florists' shipment box. Mom may help assign the right corsages to the right people, and you might find yourself assigning a friend to run the men's boutonnieres over to where the men are getting ready (this delivery slip-up happens more often than you think!).

- Make sure you have the wedding ring on you, in a safe place, ready for transport to the ceremony. (Warning: Don't slip it on your thumb for safekeeping—it might get stuck.)

- Be ready to run out for extra stockings in case of tears. Or be a savior and have a few extra pairs in your bag, just in case.
- The Maid of Honor may get the, um…honor of helping the bride affix her veil, zipping her up, and completing her look for the day.

Something Old, Something New…

…Something Borrowed, Something Blue, and a Penny for your Shoe. So goes the old adage of good luck rituals that most brides still look forward to. As part of the bridal party, you may share with the bride's mom and grandmother, the groom's mom and grandmother, and other family members the wonderful and memorable task of giving the bride her good-luck charms. She may count the dress as her something new, her mom's own wedding-day diamond pendant as her something borrowed, her grandmother's saint medallion pinned to the hem of her dress as her something old, and then something from you as her something blue (FYI: Blue is tradi-tionally the color symbolizing fidelity and loyalty). Here are some ideas to consider in the blue category:

- A blue heart or angel temporary tattoo for her to apply in a place the groom will find later
- A blue crystal good-luck charm to pin onto her bouquet handle
- A handkerchief with blue embroidery
- A garter with blue trim
- A blue toe ring
- A blue heart sticker for the sole of her shoe

Some brides get light blue nail polish for their pedicures, taking care of the something blue themselves.

- Practice arranging the bride's train and veil as you will do during the ceremony. When she has the gown on, take a moment to practice helping her turn around, with you fluffing and placing her veil neatly on the floor
- Pose for the pre-wedding pictures and video, and keep an eye on the clock so that you can depart for the wedding on time
- Give the bride a hug and lipstick-free kiss to wish her luck

14

After the Ceremony

When the ceremony is complete, you'll line up in the receiving line (if the bride wishes to have one), doing your part to keep the line moving. Shake hands, hug and kiss, and then tell chatty guests you'll catch up with them later. Maid of Honor, you may have to keep a special eye out for guests who linger too long to talk to the bride and groom. Keep the line moving, interrupt if you have to, and let the next guest approach.

Lipstick Alert

Be sure that when the receiving line starts, and throughout it, you're there to wipe lipstick from the bride's cheek, and from the groom's. While you're at it, have breath mints handy for both of them.

You may be asked to distribute those little packets of birdseed or bubble-blowing bottles for the bride and groom's send-off, or ask the Junior Brides-maid to handle that task. If doves or butterflies will be released, just enjoy the show and join the rest of the bridal party for the official post-ceremony photograph session. Again, watch the clock and keep everyone motivated and paying attention so that the pictures can be taken without you all missing the cocktail hour.

It's time to move on to the reception!

15

The Life of the Party

The best gift you can give to the bride and groom at this point is getting their reception started off on the right (high-heeled) foot. That means you can help the party be a success from start to finish. By start, I mean the first minute you walk through the ballroom doors and begin mingling with the crowd. The ceremony may be over, and there may be a lemon martini or two waiting for you at the bar, but you're not off-duty!

In this section, you'll discover just how vital you are to the fun factor of the reception.

Mix, Mingle, and Introduce. At any wedding, the room is half-full of strangers. His side doesn't know her side. Work friends don't know cousins. The first half-hour to an hour of a wedding then is full of people just talking to those at their own tables. So here is where you step in to mix, mingle, and introduce people you know to one another. The couple who knows no one at the wedding will appreciate your good hostessing, and the singles you hook up just might hit it off!

Get on the Dance Floor. Sometimes weddings get off to a slow start because all of the guests are just waiting for someone else to be first on the dance floor. That would be you. Grab the other bridesmaids or your date and be a trailblazer, filling the dance floor so that everyone else will follow your lead. The deejay or band will thank you later—you've made him or her look good too.

Request Songs. Speaking of the deejay or band, you may have to be the party rescuer if it's clear the music being played isn't suiting your crowd. Sure, the bride and groom usually submit a song playlist before the wedding, but if even they are unhappy about the songs being spun and can't get to the bandstand to request songs (because they're too busy shaking hands and accepting congratulations), it's up to you to ask for songs or music types you know will be a better match to the crowd. With just this one move, you might save the party.

Running Interference. The bride may have asked you to be her bodyguard: "If Mike comes up to me, make sure you save me." It's unfortunate, but whenever you get a few hundred relatives together, there's bound to be some dynamic of conflict somewhere in the room (Mike might be a shameless salesman in search of venture capitalists for his new startup, and never got the memo about appropriate behavior in social settings). Or you might save the day if you distance feuding exes, or keep your friend's ex-husband's new girlfriend away from her. Deft interference is done with a smile and a great distraction. Crisis averted—on to the shrimp cocktail station.

Date Etiquette. If you've brought a date to the wedding, make sure you're practicing good date etiquette. Sure, you want to be by his side, dance with him, and have a great time together, but don't isolate yourself at the table if he doesn't want to dance or ignore all other guests and activities in the room. Bounce back and forth. Bridesmaid date dilemmas have put a sour taste in many brides' mouths, especially if your date gets drunk and sloppy. Remove such offenders if it's really bad (call him a cab), and make a mental note that it's not all about him.

Give a Great Toast. Sure, the dancing and the food make for a great reception, but it's also the words spoken that give a wedding something extra special, extra personalized. If you're the Maid of Honor, you can take the microphone after the Best Man's speech and give a toast of your own. As a bridesmaid or spokeswoman for the group of bridesmaids, your toast to the bride (or the bride and groom) will add a special memory to the day. Take time before the wedding day to write out your best, funniest, and most touching toast, and then deliver it to the room with flair and confidence.

Ensure Your Comfort. Can't walk, much less dance, in those shoes? Kick them off and go barefoot, or do as the bride might do and get a second pair of comfy shoes for hours of dancing.

Create Great Moments. Every wedding has a magical quality to it, and you can add even more magic by creating special moments. Bring the flower girls out onto the dance floor with your group. The crowd will whip out their cameras, and you've made a moment. Dance with the bride's great-aunts and great-uncles. Bring the bride over to the bar for a girls' shot, a special toast just for your own little group. Dedicate a song for your group and bring the bride out to dance with you—it might be that song you always sang together in the car on road trips or the bride's favorite song. Dedicate another song to the bride and groom, inviting them out onto the dance floor for a second spotlight dance.

16

Special Reception Moments

Beyond those special, spur-of-the-moment experiences you're creating at the reception, like song dedications and unique dance partner combinations, there will be plenty of traditional special moments at the party. As unique and personalized as their wedding may be (she's one-of-a-kind, after all!), they may still have chosen several traditions to include, such as the throwing of the bouquet or the flinging of the garter.

In most of these traditions, it's your role to stand by and watch, applaud with the crowd, or help everyone to focus their attention to where the couple is cutting the cake. You're helping these special traditions to have their time in the spotlight, appreciated as they should be. Here, then, are your top tips for each special, traditional moment at the reception:

The Introduction into the Room. At many weddings, the bridal party is also introduced formally into the room by the deejay or emcee along with fun, playful music. It's your job to walk or dance into the room as instructed and then stand where placed on the dance floor so that the bride and groom can make their big entrance, for the first time anywhere, as husband and wife.

The First Dance. The bride and groom dance their dance, waltz their waltz, or tango their tango, and you stand by admiringly. Then, you may be invited to dance with your male partner in the bridal party to finish out the song. Smile for the photographer and enjoy the dance.

Toasts. As mentioned earlier, you may give a toast too, if you wish. Speak slowly, keep it short, and make it good.

Cutting the Cake. The bride and groom cut their first slice of cake and feed it to one another. They may be polite and neat about it, or it may turn into an all-out, face-smushing icing-fest. You need to know that some brides and grooms arrange ahead of time to "keep it neat and polite" at the request of their families, who would swoon and pass out if any face-smushing occurred. So don't be one of those drunk hecklers who yell at them to smear each other with icing, or boo them if they don't. They probably have an arrangement about it.

Throwing the Bouquet. "What? They're not going to throw the bouquet? I felt lucky this time! I was going to catch it!" Some bridesmaids are truly disappointed that many brides are choosing to forego this good-luck ritual (having seen enough physical injuries, fights, and shattered chandeliers at other weddings) in favor of presenting the bouquet to the couple who has been married the longest in the room. Or new creations of nosegay bouquets have been designed to split into five mini-bouquets that five of you will catch. The one with the charm on it designates "the winner."

Removing and Throwing the Garter. This practice too is often being passed over, since many couples don't like the "going up the skirt" ritual. Again, don't be surprised if you don't get the chance to sit down in front of two hundred wedding guests to have a groomsmen reach up your dress to place a garter as high up on your leg as possible. It just might not happen.

Cultural Traditions. Since weddings are planned with personalized elements, the couple's ethnic heritage may come into play. You may be lucky enough to witness or even take part in a cultural tradition, such as presenting the bride and groom with bread, salt, and wine as good luck items. Take these rituals very seriously; other guests in the room certainly are. It's a bad move to show confusion or judgment on any ritual you don't understand. "The Chicken Dance" and a line dance may or may not be played. Try not to show your despair over this.

17

Your Must-Have Pictures from the Reception

The pictures you take at the reception are certain to be more relaxed, fun, and personality-revealing than that lineup of posed pictures taken before the ceremony. So have fun with it! Grab that wedding photographer, use your own digital camera, or make good use of those throwaway cameras from the guest tables and capture this once-in-a-lifetime day in style. These pictures will be so valuable to you that you may even copy the best ones to give to the bride and other bridesmaids, or enlarge them and frame them to give out as gifts in the future.

Here are the must-have shots you'll want from the reception:

- The bride with all the bridesmaids lifting champagne glasses in a toast and laughing.
- The bride and groom with all the bridesmaids, laughing, dancing, or sharing a toast.
- All the bridesmaids with all the groomsmen.
- All the bridesmaids with their dates.
- All of you dancing as a group.

- That girls' shot toast at the bar, with each of you lifting up your glasses.
- Individual shots of each bridesmaid together with the bride.
- The first group hug with the bride.
- Shots of you making the most of the wedding's location, like all of you standing on the edge of a big fountain on the estate's grounds or all of you splashing in the edge of the ocean's surf, holding your dresses out of the water.
- A walking-away shot of all of you with the bride, such as the group of you walking away from the camera along the beach or in a garden. This type of artsy shot becomes a favorite, as it shows off that great plunging backline of your dress and gives that "we'll always walk together" into the sunset kind of image.
- A shot of just your hands (featuring the bride's new wedding band) holding up your champagne glasses in a toast.
- All of your names written in the sand at a beach wedding, along with a special message like "Good luck Sarah and Mark, Love...(all your names)." Makes a great gift to the couple later.
- Along the same lines, a shot of all of you holding up a sign you've made: "Good luck Sarah and Mark! We love you!" You'll be holding up your glasses in a toast, and this picture becomes a great keepsake for the bride and groom from you.

- Of course, be sure to get great solo shots of just you. Close-up and full-length. You look terrific, so get a fabulous picture of you that you can frame and give to your boyfriend or husband to keep on his desk at work. Or use this picture for your online dating site profile as many single bridesmaids do. Pretty soon, that picture could be on your special someone's desk at work.

Figure out the best, most personalized shots you want of your group and make a note to capture them. Look for special moments and make great use of the scenery, such as a colorful sunset or fall foliage on the trees, an illuminated fountain, or the lights of the cityscape in the distance.

With digital cameras, you can upload your favorites right away, email them to each other and even get assorted gift items like mugs, magnets, and tee shirts sporting your favorite photo.

Part Six

After the Reception

18

Closing Down the Party

The party's over when the house lights come up, the deejay says goodnight, and the bartender stops pouring the drinks. As the last remaining business of paying the site manager and tipping everyone from the bartender to the coat check attendant takes place, you have some cleanup duty as well.

You might start by helping to usher straggling guests out to the parking lot—calling them cabs if need be—and recommending a great lounge where they can go to continue the evening (more on that in a minute). However, your main task is cleanup. Here are ways you can pitch in to close down the party well:

- Help carry the bride and groom's wedding gifts out to the car.
- Retrieve the guest book and make sure it gets transported back with the gifts.
- Retrieve the basket of throwaway cameras, or take them from each guest table, and send those home with the gifts or give them to the person who's taken on film-developing duty.
- Look for anything that's been left behind by guests, such as jackets, cameras, sunglasses, even

purses, and give them to the bride's parents for safekeeping (that's who guests will call, not the site manager). Look in the coat-check closet for any coats that have been left behind as well.

- Help clean the site up, if necessary.
- Supervise the packing of any rented items, if necessary.

And of course, there's courtesy:

- Thank the bride and groom's parents for a terrific party. Comment on how much everyone appreciated it and how terrific the event was.
- Thank the site staff, including the manager, servers, bartenders, and others who helped make the event extra special. Your moment of gratitude will mean so much to them.
- Thank the musicians who are packing up their equipment. If they did a great job, they deserve to hear thanks too.

Decorating the Bride and Groom's Getaway Car

If your group will enact the traditional decorating of the bride and groom's getaway car, you might sneak out of the reception during a slow dance and put flower garlands on the car, along with a "Just Married" placard on their back bumper (or inside their back window). If you have keys to their car, you can put flowers or a gift and card inside their car for their getaway. Shoes and cans are no longer tied to bumpers, and little "Just Married" signs with metal clasps have been known to scratch car paint as they flap in the wind during driving, so steer clear of those options. Check party supply stores for safe window paints and temporary stick-on window decals that say "Just Married."

And now, it's on to the after party!

19

The After Party

Once the reception has completely shut down, then it may be time for you, the bride and groom, and other select guests to continue on to the next party of the evening, the after party. This trend is so hot that couples are planning it like a third official part of the big day. They're hiring caterers and musicians to make this smaller, more casual, and intimate party something spectacular.

The most common form of after party is heading back to the home or hotel room of a relative or friend for a relaxed evening of wine and snacks. Everyone gets to kick off their shoes and perhaps even change into more comfortable clothes. Or, if it's a pool or hot tub party, as may be the case, bathing suits and flip-flops. (A party in a hotel room right there at the site prevents guests who have been drinking from having to drive, and they can just walk right to their own rooms afterwards. As always, it's safety first.)

If you'll head out to a bar or jazz club, decide if you all want to remain in your bridesmaids' dresses (which single bridesmaids tell me always garners them plenty of attention from other bar patrons!) or change into your own going-out clothes.

Other ideas for the after party:

- Going to a cigar bar
- Going to a sports bar
- Going to a gourmet dessert restaurant for treats and espresso
- Going out for ice cream
- Heading out to the beach to relax and await the sunrise
- Partying in the hotel room or suite, sometimes the parents' suite
- Just heading home for pizza and drinks, perhaps a movie night or game night

If you're planning the after party, make sure you specify who is invited. Send out email invites (at www.evite.com), and get RSVPs so that you can create a memorable party, and check back to Part Three for party ideas that would be ideal for this get-together. The bride and groom might even wish to join you, as so many do nowadays. Hey, the night is young. Make the most of it!

20

While the Bride and Groom Are Away

You've sent them off with your congratulations, hugs, kisses, and thanks for letting you share their day with them. Now, while they're away on their honeymoon, you can make their welcome home something special as well. As the dear loved one you are, you'll surprise them when they walk in the door and drop their luggage, ready to start their married life back in the real world. Here's how to make it special:

- Be sure you've taken care of everything they entrusted to you while they are away. You've house-sat for them, taken care of their pets, watered their plants, and now they'll come home to a spotless house and a well-fed Fido.
- If you've taken in their mail, be sure you've kept it all in a basket on their kitchen table where it will be organized and ready for their review.
- Set their bedroom up as a love den. Set out candles (unlit for safety, of course!), sprinkle rose petals on their bed, set up vases of flowers, lay out new silk robes for them, and put a chocolate

mint on each of their pillows. That's a romantic surprise the groom may even take credit for
(he'll owe you later!).

· Fill their refrigerator with gourmet goodies,
snacks, a bowl of fresh strawberries, a great bottle of wine, and a luscious dessert like a chocolate mousse cake. Not having to go food
shopping that day is a gift in itself.

· Set out new bubble baths and bath oils by
their tub.

· Set out vases of flowers all over their home: in
the entryway, the kitchen, and the living room.

· Have the throwaway camera photos developed
and leave them out where the couple can
immediately go through them. They've been
waiting a while.

· If you have video footage of their wedding day,
set up their VCR with the tape and a note to
"Press Play."

· Together with the bridesmaids, leave a terrific
"Welcome Home" message for them on their
voice mail. Perhaps from the after party they
missed.

· And, of course, you might plan a welcome home
dinner upon their return, so they can see all of
you and share their honeymoon stories over some
great wine and great food and great company.

A Note from the Author

You're going to do a terrific job as a bridesmaid, and even more important, you're going to pay great honor to your relationship with the bride. Not too often in life do we get "chosen" in a very public way as being very special to someone we love, so make the most of the opportunity. Find amazing ways to let the bride know you love her in return.

I welcome you to share your stories with me for future editions of this book. Tell me about all the great things you planned for the shower, about how you defused a potentially hazardous situation with a control-freak bridesmaid, how you turned a wedding fiasco into the best time anyone's ever had. Visit me at www.sharonnaylor.net to submit your stories, and you'll in turn help thousands of future bridesmaids follow your example.

Thank you for letting me guide you through your experience as a bridesmaid.

All the best,
Sharon Naylor

Resources

(Note: This collection of resources is purely for your research use only. Neither the author nor the publisher endorses any particular company or website. In addition, due to the constant changing of website URLs and phone numbers, we apologize if any company or site has changed their contact information since the writing of this book.)

Bridesmaids' Gowns

After Six: 800-444-8304, www.aftersix.com

Alfred Angelo: 800-531-1125, www.alfredangelo.com

Bill Levkoff: 800-LEVKOFF, www.billlevkoff.com

Chadwick's of Boston Special Occasions: 800-525-6650, www.chadwicks.com

Champagne Formals: www.champagneformals.com

David's Bridal: 888-480-BRIDE, www.davidsbridal.com

Dessy Creations: www.dessy.com

Galina: 212-564-1020, www.galinabridals.com

Group USA: 866-226-0622, www.groupusa.com

JC Penney: 877-407-6966, www.jcpenney.com

Jessica McClintock: 800-322-1189,
www.jessicamcclintock.com

Jim Hjelm Occasions: 800-686-7880,
www.jimhjelmoccasions.com

Lazaro: 212-764-5781, www.lazarobridal.com

Macy's: 888-269-3187,
www.macys.weddingchannel.com

Melissa Sweet Bridal Collection: 404-633-4395,
www.melissasweet.com

Mori Lee: 212-840-5070, www.morileeinc.com

Roaman's Romance (plus sizes): 800-436-0800,
www.roamans.com

Sihouettes: www.silhouettesmaids.com

Spiegel: 800-527-1577, www.spiegel.com

Vera Wang: 800-VEW-VERA, www.verawang.com

Watters and Watters: 972-960-9884, www.watters.com

Wedding Channel: www.weddingchannel.com

Department Stores for Dresses and Lingerie
Bloomingdales: www.bloomingdales.com

JC Penney: 800-222-6161, www.jcpenney.com

Lord and Taylor: www.lordandtaylor.com

Macy's: www.macys.com

Spiegel: 800-SPIEGEL, www.spiegel.com

Victoria's Secret: www.victoriassecret.com

Shoes and Handbags
Bloomingdales: www.bloomingdales.com

Kenneth Cole: 800-KENCOLE,
www.kennethcole.com

Dyeables: 800-431-2000, www.dyeables.com

Fenaroli for Regalia: 617-350-6556,
www.fenaroli.com

Macy's: www.macys.com

Nicole Miller: www.nicolemiller.com

Nina Footwear: www.ninashoes.com

Payless Shoe Source: www.payless.com

Salon Shoes: 650-588-8677, www.salonshoes.com

Target: 800-800-8800, www.target.com

Watters and Watters: 972-960-9884,
www.watters.com

Beauty Supplies

Avon: www.avon.com

Bobbi Brown Essentials: www.bobbibrown.com

Clinique: www.clinique.com

Elizabeth Arden: www.elizabetharden.com

Estee Lauder: www.esteelauder.com

Eve: www.eve.com

iBeauty: www.ibeauty.com

Lancome: www.lancome.com

Laura Geller: www.laurageller.com

L'Oreal: www.loreal.com

Mac: www.maccosmetics.com

Makeover Studio: www.makeoverstudio.com
(choose your face shape and experiment
with makeup shades and looks)

Max Factor: www.maxfactor.com

Maybelline: www.maybelline.com

Neutrogena: www.neutrogena.com

Pantene: www.pantene.com

Reflect.com (customized beauty products):
  www.reflect.com

Rembrandt (tooth-whitening products):
  www.rembrandt.com

Revlon: www.revlon.com

Sephora: www.sephora.com

Cake Supplies
Wilton: 800-794-5866, www.wilton.com

Wine and Champagne
Wine.com: www.wine.com

Wine Searcher: www.winesearcher.com

Wine Spectator: www.winespectator.com

Paper Supplies
OfficeMax: 800-283-7674, www.officemax.com

Paper Access: 800-727-3701,
  www.paperaccess.com

Paper Direct: 800-A-PAPERS,
  www.paperdirect.com

Staples: 800-3STAPLE, www.staples.com

USA BRIDE: 978-922-1213, www.usabride.com

Ultimate Wedding Store: 800-300-5587,
  www.ultimatewedding.com/store

Wedmart.com: 888-802-2229, www.wedmart.com

Williams Sonoma: 800-541-2376,
  www.williams-sonoma.com

Books and Planners

Amazon.com: www.amazon.com
Barnes and Noble: 800-843-2665, www.bn.com
Borders: www.borders.com

Warehouse Stores:

BJ's Wholesale: www.bjs.com
Costco: www.costco.com
Sam's Club: www.samsclub.com

Cameras

C&G Disposable Cameras: 888-431-3463,
   www.cngdisposablecamera.com
Kodak: 800-242-2424, www.kodak.com

Favors and Gifts

Beverly Clark Collection: 800-888-6866,
   www.beverlyclark.com
Chandler's Candle Company: 800-463-7143,
   www.chandlerscandle.com
Charming Favors: www.charmingfavors.com
Double T Limited: www.uniquefavors.com
Eve.com: www.eve.com
Exclusively Weddings: 800-759-7666,
   www.exclusivelyweddings.com
Favors by Serendipity: 800-320-2664,
   www.favorsbyserendipity.com
Forever and Always Company: 800-404-4025,
   www.foreverandalways.com
Gift Emporia.com: www.giftemporia.com

Godiva: 800-9-GODIVA, www.godiva.com

Gratitude: 800-914-4342, www.giftsofgratitude.com

Illuminations: www.illuminations.com

Michael's: www.michaels.com

Oriental Trading Company: 800-875-8480,
www.orientaltrading.com

Pier 1 Imports: www.pier1.com

Service Merchandise: 866-978-2583

Shari's Berries (chocolate-covered strawberries):
877-BERRIES, www.berries.com

Things Remembered: 866-902-4438,
www.thingsremembered.com

Tree and Floral Beginnings (seedlings, bulbs, and
candles) 888-315-7333, www.plantamemory.com

Wedding Accessories: www.weddingaccessories.net

Victoria's Secret: 800-888-8200,
www.victoriassecret.com

Wireless: 800-669-9999, www.wireless2.com

Wedding Registries

Bed Bath and Beyond: 800-GO-BEYOND,
www.bedbathandbeyond.com

Bloomingdales: 800-888-2WED,
www.bloomingdales.com

Bon Ton: 800-9BONTON, www.bonton.com

Crate and Barrel: 800-967-6696,
www.crateandbarrel.com

Dillards: 800-626-6001, www.dillards.com

Filene's: www.FilenesWeddings.com

Fortunoff: 800-777-2807, www.fortunoff.com

Gift Emporia.com: www.giftemporia.com

Gump's: www.gumps.com

Hecht's: www.hechts.com

Home Depot: www.homedepot.com

HoneyLuna (honeymoon registry):
   800-809-5862, www.honeyluna.com

JC Penney: 800-JCP-GIFT, www.jcpgift.com

Justgive.org

Kohl's: 800-837-1500, www.kohls.com

Linens 'n Things: www.lnt.com

Macy's Wedding Channel: 888-92-BRIDES,
   www.macys.weddingchannel.com

National Bridal Service: www.nationalbridal.com

Neiman Marcus: www.neimanmarcus.com

Pier 1 Imports: 800-245-4595, www.pier1.com

REI: www.rei.com

Sears: www.sears.com

Service Merchandise: 866-978-2583,
   www.servicemerchandise.com

Sur La Table: 800-243-0852, www.surlatable.com

Target's Club Wedd Gift Registry: 800-888-9333,
   www.target.com

The Gift: www.thegift.com

The Wedding List: 800-345-7795,
   www.theweddinglist.com

Tiffany & Co.: 800-526-0649, www.tiffany.com

Ultimate Online Wedding Mall:
   www.ultimateweddingmall.com

Wedding Channel: www.weddingchannel.com

Wedding Network (Internet wedding registry):
  www.weddingnetwork.com
Williams Sonoma: 800-541-2376,
  www.williams-sonoma.com

Personalized Wedding Websites
Wed Studio: www.wedstudio.com

Index